Lillia
Jennifer Too

FORTUNE & FENG SHUI

2021

KONSEPBOOKS
ASTROLOGY . FENG SHUI . INSPIRATIONS

Fortune & Feng Shui 2021 Sheep

by *Lillian Too* and *Jennifer Too*

Published by KONSEP LAGENDA SDN BHD (223 855)
Kuala Lumpur 59100 Malaysia

For more Konsep books, go to *www.lillian-too.com* or *www.wofs.com*
To report errors, please send a note to errors@konsepbooks.com
For general feedback, email feedback@konsepbooks.com

ISBN 978-967-2929-00-0
Published in Malaysia, September 2020

SHEEP 2021

BIRTH YEAR	WESTERN CALENDAR DATES	AGE	KUA NUMBER MALES	KUA NUMBER FEMALES
Metal Sheep	17 Feb 1931 - 5 Feb 1932	90	6 West Group	9 East Group
Water Sheep	5 Feb 1943 - 24 Jan 1944	78	3 East Group	3 East Group
Wood Sheep	24 Jan 1955 - 11 Feb 1956	66	9 East Group	6 West Group
Fire Sheep	9 Feb 1967 - 29 Jan 1968	54	6 West Group	9 East Group
Earth Sheep	28 Jan 1979 - 15 Feb 1980	42	3 East Group	3 East Group
Metal Sheep	15 Feb 1991 - 3 Feb 1992	30	9 East Group	6 West Group
Water Sheep	1 Feb 2003 - 21 Jan 2004	18	6 West Group	9 East Group
Wood Sheep	19 Feb 2015 - 7 Feb 2016	6	3 East Group	3 East Group

Cover Art by Josh Yeo Zhu Lin

Features a striking Sheep on hilly pastures lit by a magnificent sun, a nod to the romantic flair of this alluring sign. In 2021, the Sheep enjoys Big Auspicious luck, bringing the promise of catching a meaningful break.

CONTENTS

Chapter One

Chapter Two

very auspicious as the Tiger is the sign that brings hidden wealth to the year.

Each year we design a wallet to vibrate and sync with the energies of the year, and for 2021, our wealth wallet features the stock market bull. It is the Year of the Ox and the Wall Street Bull is a most auspicious symbolic cousin of the sign of the year. The Wall Street Bull represents your investments going up, and your asset wealth growing.

We also have the **Asset Wealth Bull with Wealth Amulet** which will attract wealth-generating luck to any home which invites it in. Display prominently in the West where the *Star of Current Prosperity* has flown to this year or on your desk in front of you where you work. The idea is to see it daily and its subliminal effects will magically influence your actions and ability to attract wealth luck into your life.

WOOD *brings growth*

WOOD is the element that stands for growth. In 2021, it also signifies intelligence and creativity. It is what brings fresh new ideas to the mix, encouraging a blossoming of imagination and ingenuity. As we foray further into the new decade, old ideas will increasingly lose appeal and old technologies become obsolete with increasing speed. These need to be replaced and they will, and it will be those who can dream up the new ideas, methods, designs and technologies that will profit.

For the individual looking at making it in a rapidly changing world, it will be enhanced creativity and thinking outside the box that will help you. Surround yourself with the vibrant energy of plants and greenery, invite fresh flowers displayed in auspicious vases into your living space. If you live in a modern skyscraper city where feasting on green is difficult or unusual, look for ways to introduce indoor gardens into your home and office space, take regular time to visit parks and gardens, or make time to visit the countryside to refuel and recharge your senses with the power of nature.

THE COLOR GREEN – Greens of all kinds represent innovation and vision in 2021. Fill your wardrobe with lots of this color in emerald green, lime green, neon green, shamrock, chartreuse, sage, seafoam… all of these will inject your wardrobe with a fresh dash of inspiration and will attract wonderfully inspired energies into your aura. Green this year is very lucky and brings to the wearer a new lease of life. If you have been feeling dull, uninspired or at a crossroads, introducing a pop of bright green into what you wear or carry will give you the boost you need to change track, get moving, get started. It is the "energizing" colour of the year and should be made use of liberally and profusely.

TEND TO YOUR GARDEN:
There's nothing that invokes better yang Wood energy than thriving plants and greenery. Make a trip to your local nursery and bring home some vibrant new plants to add to your garden. If you live in an apartment, introduce some live potted plants into your living space. This will stir up the creative juices in you needed to dream up new ideas and to hatch ingenious strategies for your work and in your life.

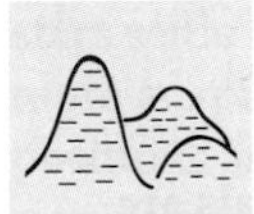

EARTH *brings power & influence*

EARTH in the Year of the Ox is the intrinsic element of the animal sign of the year. It is the element that symbolizes stability, strength and permanence. It is the element that ensures that however crazy the energy gets, however quickly the world changes around us, we can dig our heels deep and stay grounded with our values and our visions intact. Earth energy will prevent us being light-eared and light-headed, or easily influenced. In 2021, the element of EARTH also signifies recognition and power. It brings the luck of rank and position, and boosts one's chances when it comes to promotion and upward mobility, whether in one's career or in any climb to the top of any organization. Earth energy brings you influence and command and will make people listen to you.

EARTH COLORS – Wearing shades of earth tones brings you respect and makes people listen to you. It keeps you rational and well-balanced and envelops you with an aura of dependability. An excellent color group to use when you need others to take you seriously. Earth colors include yellow, orange, beige and cream, in all their shades. Wear such colors when you feel you need others to take notice of you, when you want to boost your influence over others and when you need people to listen to you. Those of you ambitious for your career to get a boost will benefit greatly from making use of earth colors.

realize big ambitions they may have been harboring. For these signs, opportunities will be plentiful. Success comes for those who are hungry and resolute. Remember that this year, results do not come immediately, so one must not get discouraged if the path to actualization seems long or even impossible. The winners will be those with the staying power to keep at it and stay the course. Hold on to your dreams, and don't change your mind at every setback. Trust in your instincts and passions, and don't give power to those who disturb your mind or pour cold water on your ideas.

While the Stars of Big Auspicious bring really fabulous blessings, so do the Stars of Small Auspicious. These have the same effect as their big brother stars, but they bring success in smaller measures and in stages. The signs enjoying Small Auspicious this year are the **Ox**, **Tiger**, **Dog** and **Boar.** For these signs, they are likely

to meet with small successes that form the stepping stones to bigger success later on. For these signs, this is a year for building firm foundations and laying out the pathway for future triumphs.

Small Auspicious brings end goals that hold slightly longer time trajectories, but accompanied with the same staying power, success does ultimately come. Learn to celebrate the smallest of wins and stay clearheaded about your ultimate goals. If you constantly step back to examine the bigger picture, you will not lose sight of why you are doing what you're doing.

ENHANCER: Remember that *Stars of Big and Small Auspicious* bring the potential of great fortune, but to enjoy their benefits to the fullest, they need to be enhanced. Each year then, we design a Big Auspicious Enhancer to kickstart the very positive effects of these stars. This year, all animal signs benefit from displaying the **Six Birds Auspicious Multiplier**. This activator featuring an I-Ching coin with six birds and the auspicious amulet enhancer brings new opportunities. The 6 birds activates the #6 Heaven Star that rules the year's Lo Shu chart. The number 6 is the number of the heavens, which unlocks the celestial hand of the Gods. Display this potent activator in a place where you can see it often – either in a prominent place in the home, or in front of you on your work desk.

6 Birds Auspicious Multiplier. Unlocks the Big Auspicious luck of the year.

LUCK FROM THE HEAVENS

Two stars that further magnify the luck of the heavens are the *Golden Deity Star* and the *Star of the Heavenly Seal*. These land in the location of the **Horse** and the **Monkey**, bringing these two signs the luck of celestial fortunes. For these two signs, help comes without having to seek it. They enjoy the patronage of powerful mentors with many wishing to help them. They also have better instincts and can trust their own judgment more. For the Horse, as it also enjoys two Big Auspicious stars, little can go wrong as long as it stays judicious and diligent. The Monkey however needs to employ its trademark cunning to make the most of the Heaven Seal; it has to dodge the Yin House and Facing 3 Killings, but its main 24 Mountain star influence is extremely positive.

To make the most of these stars, we recommend that the Horse and Monkey invite in a **Golden Deity** into the home. Any Buddha, God or holy figure in line with your own faith will work. We particularly love **Kuan Yin, the Goddess of Mercy**, revered by Chinese all around the world. She is the female personification of the compassionate Buddha and brings wealth, health and happiness and protection from harm.

Kuan Yin

THE GENERAL STAR

The **Rooster** enjoys the General Star, which brings it power and authority, but unfortunately also fuels its short fuse and hot temper. But the Rooster this year has the very lucky #8 star, which enhances its fortunes and intrinsic energy. The Rooster as a sign does not suffer fool's gladly, so all these indications point to a Rooster that reigns supreme in 2021, but one who may be insufferable to those it considers "beneath" them, whether in intelligence or in status. To make the most of this star, all Roosters this year benefit from displaying the **Power Ru Yi**, the scepter of authority which boosts its command as boss or leader, while ensuring no disgruntled subordinates try to make trouble, or rivals rise up to try to displace it.

Star of the Yin House

This star brings danger of sickness and disease, and a general lack of energy to those it afflicts. It is particularly dangerous if one is already ill or elderly, or with other heavy afflictions indicated in their charts. This year, there are two Yin House stars and these arrive in the SW and North, affecting the **Sheep**, **Monkey** and **Rat**. All three of these signs are advised to take more care this year when it comes to health, well-being and safety. We strongly suggest that these signs carry protective amulets to shield them from the influence of malevolent spirits that may wreak havoc in their lives. Any of the **seed syllables Om, Ah or**

Hum will invoke the presence of the mighty Buddha, establishing a firm spiritual circumference of protection around the wearer.

If ill health is of particular concern, we recommend wearing and displaying Health Amulets. The **Wu Lou**, **Garuda Bird**, and the **Healing Deer**, bring precious cosmic protection. The deer is especially wonderful; this animal has always been associated with health, strength and vigor. It is also the animal that holds the solution to good health when all other methods have not seemed to work. There are many folk legends associated with the deer in all cultures, but in Chinese mythology, the deer is almost always shown accompanying Sau, the divine God of Longevity.

Healing Deer

The Robbery Star

This star brings money loss and betrayal and especially affects the **Tiger** in 2021. Those born under this sign need to be especially mindful not to get taken in by con men and getting cheated by others. There is higher chance of getting conned into undertaking bad investments. Business partners and associates could prove untrustworthy. It is also very important whenever one has this affliction to take care of personal safety. Robberies, muggings, petty thieves and street crime become more of a danger. This star also brings risk of becoming a victim of chance or collateral damage in somebody else's fight.

To counter this negative star, you need the image of the **Blue Rhino and Elephant** in the home, and you MUST carry the **Anti Robbery Amulet**. This protects against losing money and possessions. It is also important to protect against personal harm and injury; wear protective amulet at all times! Females in particular should avoid venturing out alone late at night or putting themselves under unnecessary risk; they should carry the **Nightspot Protection Amulet** for protection against petty crime.

Yearly Conflict & Yearly Killings

These stars bring obstacles to everything you do, making it difficult to make meaningful progress. These are the stars that can discourage you from remaining steadfast and keeping on your intended path. It throws up unexpected snags and hitches, and when left unchecked, can overwhelm one with feelings of depression and anxiety. These are negative stars that gather the slings and arrows of misfortune hurling them your way with some measure of ferocity. It is as such extremely important to take note of their location each year and take definite steps to neutralize them.

In 2021, the Yearly Killings star has landed in the **Dragon**'s location of SE1, and the Yearly Conflict Star visits the N3 sector, affecting the animal signs of **Rat** and **Ox**.

The *Yearly Killings Star* is deadlier and needs immediate action – we suggest that all Dragon-born and all those whose bedrooms or main door location are in the SE carry the **28 Hums Protection Wheel** and invite in the **Buddha image of Nangsi Zilnon Guru Rinpoche**. He is the warrior Buddha who completely overcomes all types of obstacles brought by the Yearly Killings.

28 Hums Protection Wheel

The *Yearly Conflict Star* makes everyone want to fight with you, bringing opposition to your ideas and making it difficult to see your projects through. Working in teams becomes especially difficult. At work, this could mean difficult colleagues and fierce politicking by workplace rivals. Those afflicted by this star could find themselves spending the better part of their time dodging potshots rather than focusing on their work. It makes work life very unpleasant, and the effects of this star can also permeate one's social and private life. This negative star arrives in the N3 sector affecting all whose main door or bedroom or office are located in this part of the home or office, and it affects Rat and Ox born people. Those affected by this affliction need to carry protection amulets and display the relevant cures. The **Dorje Drolo Scorpion Amulet** is especially helpful in this regard.

Natural Disaster Star

This star arrives in the East sector, affecting those who spend much time in this part of the home. This is the star that puts in you in harm's way – being at the wrong place at the wrong time. It brings all manner of natural misfortune including floods, fires, earthquakes, tsunamis, viruses and disease. If you are afflicted by this star, you MUST carry spiritual protection. ALL East-facing homes benefit from inviting in a statue of **Guru Rinpoche**, and all living in homes facing East should wear the **Bhrum Pendant** which protects against all kinds of harm, illness, accidents and avoidable misfortune.

LUCK OF THE 12 ANIMAL SIGNS

Every animal sign is affected by a host of factors which change each year, producing a different basket of combinations which influence each individual sign's luck differently. Aside from the animal sign year you were born under, there are additional factors affecting your luck, but viewed together with these indications, anyone can alter the course of their lives and make intelligent decisions to maximize luck through any given year.

Here we summarize the broad outlook for the different animal signs, and in later chapters of this book, we go into greater depth and detail on what all of this means for you personally, depending on your heavenly stem, your home direction, your lunar mansion and your compatibilities.

The **HORSE** is blessed with extremely fortunate indications with the double *stars of Big Auspicious* and the *Star of Golden Deity* brought by the 24 Mountains Compass of 2021. This sign has great good fortune coming, which should more than make up for the unfortunate stars it had to endure in the last two years. The Horse is an energetic and restless sign full of passion and appetite for adventure, but the last couple of years will have made it difficult for it to pursue its desires. This year changes all of this; the Horse person will feel like a cloud has lifted, and as the year progresses, things get better and better. There are no unlucky indications at all, and the Victory Star #1 promises some very exciting new developments in the Horse's life.

The Horse should boost its fortunes with the **6 Birds Auspicious Multiplier** and benefits from displaying the **Desktop Flag of Victory** in its vicinity.

Desktop Flag of Victory

The **MONKEY** and **ROOSTER** are the signs enjoying the luckiest element luck indications. These two Metal signs have superlative Life Force and Spirit Essence, suggesting an inner determination that is unwavering. These signs know exactly what it is they want and how to go about getting it. Both Monkey and Rooster are known for their innate intelligence and ingenuity, and their already immense brainpower gets a big boost this year. The Monkey in particular enjoys very promising "success" luck; not only can it get what it wants, it receives plenty of recognition to go along with it too!

The **Rooster** can boost success luck by surrounding itself with the presence of the **Victorious Windhorse Carrying a Jewel**, as can the Monkey. Both these signs also have excellent indications from the 24 Mountains, with Monkey enjoying the *Heaven Seal* and Rooster benefitting from the *General Star*. The Monkey should carry the **Dragon Heavenly Seal Amulet** and the Rooster needs the **Ru Yi**.

The sign that gets hit by the *Five Yellow* this year are the **DRAGON** and **SNAKE**. This indicates that these signs need to watch that the *wu wang* does not bring misfortune their way. The Five Yellow of 2021 sits in a Wood sector, which suggests it is NOT a deadly Five Yellow; nevertheless, the obstacles it brings can cause life to feel very unpleasant indeed and it should be strongly subdued.

Dragon and Snake this year need to carry the **Five Element Pagoda Amulet with Tree of Life** to combat the afflictive energy, turning obstacles into productive challenges, and transforming unfortunate outcomes into promising ones. Both Dragon and Snake are signs that thrive in adversity, gaining strength and shrewdness when the going gets tough. And the *wu wang* of this year can be metamorphosed into positive rather than negative results. The Snake should have the **6 Birds Auspicious Multiplier**, while the Dragon needs the **28 Hums Protection Wheel**.

The WOOD ELEMENT SIGNS of **TIGER** and **RABBIT** both enjoy very good element indications but need to boost success luck with the **Victorious Windhorse** this year. The Tiger benefits from the *Small Auspicious*, and direct access to the hidden wealth of the year, but the Rabbit needs to do more work to boost its prosperity potential. The Tiger should display the **6 Birds Auspicious Multiplier** while the Rabbit MUST carry the **Three Celestial Shields Amulet** to stay protected against the 3 Killings affliction that affects it this year.

The WATER ELEMENT SIGNS of **RAT** and **BOAR** are the most unfortunate in terms of element luck, facing very bad life force and spirit essence. This can cause a sudden lack of confidence in one's own abilities and make these two signs prone to being easily discouraged. What the Rat and Boar need this year are strong cures to lift their inner energies. They need to carry the **Life Force Amulet** and **"Om" Dakini Spirit Enhancing Amulet**. What these two signs do have however are a shared *Big Auspicious Star*. Rat and Boar working together can produce very favourable results, and their affinity with each other gets enhanced this year. These two signs will make good business partners. Of the two, Rat will be luckier than Boar, and should take the lead in any endeavor they embark on together.

"Om" Dakini Spirit Enhancing Amulet

The EARTH SIGNS of **OX**, **DOG**, **DRAGON** and **SHEEP** all have good life force but bad spirit essence. This suggests that for these signs, they have decent inherent energy, but exposure to the wrong company could be harmful to their mindsets and their motivation levels. They are spiritually weaker than usual and need to carry the **"Om" Dakini Spirit Enhancing Amulet**. Those who are spiritual in nature can draw strength from their belief systems and find solace and comfort in their spiritual practice.

The **SHEEP** meanwhile is also in direct clash with the TAI SUI of the year, and hence the priority for this sign should be to take all steps to appease the God of the Year. The Sheep needs the **Tai Sui Amulet**, and its celestial guardian animal this year should be the **Dragon Pi Yao**. The Sheep can lean on its special friend the Horse, who enjoys superlative luck in 2021. The Sheep working or hanging out with a Horse in the coming year will benefit tremendously from its astrological soulmate. But all four Earth signs are in direct or indirect conflict with the Year God and should thus ALL carry the **Tai Sui Amulet** and have his plaque in the home.

WEALTH LUCK IN 2021

Wealth luck this coming year is weak. It will be difficult to make quick money. Wealth that gets created will come from hard work rather than speculative gains. The year continues to see much disruption to the way business is done, making things difficult for those in sunset industries. Individuals who can spot new opportunities can profit, but increasingly, the free flow of information will reduce the time window for monopolies in new industries. It will be creativity and originality, together with consistent hard work that will allow individuals and businesses to generate income in 2021.

As machines take over more and more jobs, those who do not do something and stubbornly hang on to an old way of life could quickly find themselves being made redundant. The year will not be an easy one for wealth creation, and macro level events continue to depress the immediate outlook.

Certain animal signs will have element luck in their favour when it comes to wealth luck this year; even so, the advice is to weigh all decisions carefully before making them. This is a year when one can take risks, but do not put all your eggs in one basket. Make sure any risks taken are calculated ones backed by understanding and research.

WEALTH ENHANCER: All individuals benefit from inviting in wealth enhancers, particularly the **Asset Wealth Bull** which boosts money and income luck, but also protects against your assets losing value. Those invested in the stock market would benefit greatly from the presence of this bull in the home. It has been designed to look like the stock market bull on Wall Street and carries the meaning "May the market bull for you"; it also features auspicious symbols of good fortune, a red saddle to represent prosperity in 2021, and it is shown presiding over a pile of coins and ingots, signifying its control and dominance over cash. With this bull, you will always have enough money, and even those who sustain losses will quickly make it back.

GETTING YOUR TIMING RIGHT:
The Sheep in 2021 benefits from carrying the **"Green Dragon" Constellation Lucky Charms.** Comprising the 7 Sky Animals from the Dragon Constellation of the Lunar Mansions, it generates all the positive attributes of the Dragon – Courage, Charisma, Strength, Ambition, and most of all, Energy. The Sheep has mixed element luck this year, and activating the Dragon's Lunar Constellation will ensure you have the vigour and vitality to advantage from the opportunities that come your way. Keeping these charms close will also help you get your timing right when making important decisions and when acting on them.

Green Dragon Constellation Lucky Charms.

LOVE LUCK IN 2021

SINGLES CAN FIND LOVE IN 2021

For singles, this is a promising year for romance. The *Peach Blossom Star* has settled into the East, a WOOD sector, which gives it strength. The East is also the palace of the Rabbit, which is associated with the Moon and Moon Goddess who presides over fortunes related to love and romance. She bestows wishes to do with relationships, aids in matchmaking soulmates, and improves relations between married couples.

In 2021, the East becomes the place of the "Moon Rabbit" and enhancing this sector manifests love and romance for those looking for true love in their lives. Those wishing to settle down and get married, or searching for their soulmate or one true love, displaying the **Rabbit in the Moon** in the East will manifest this kind of luck for you.

MARRIED COUPLES BEWARE!!!

While there will be plenty of love and romance in 2021, it will not always be the kind that brings happiness. The year's chart also features the *Flower of Romance Star*. Unfortunately, it is the "external" version of this star – making all marriages vulnerable as there will be too much temptation from outside. Innocent flirtations can get out of hand, after-work drinks with colleagues or out-of-town business conferences can lead to inappropriate entanglements, spouses with the seven-year itch could be tempted to act on it. This is a year when those who are married should pay more attention to their other halves.

The *External Star of Romance* often affect those who have grown to take their marriage for granted. As long as you realise it, you can start taking measures to make things right. But what if an affair has already started?

CURE: We advise that when this troublesome star is present, married couples should make an effort to display symbols of marital stability and happiness in the home. All married couples should have the **Marriage Happiness Ducks** in the home, in the SW, East or center. Each can also carry the **Enhancing Relationships Amulet** to protect against third parties elbowing their way in and "crowding" the marriage.

Displaying the **"Rabbit in the Moon" Love Enhancer** in the home is also an excellent protective measure against stars that affect marital peace and happiness. In 2021, all couples can safeguard their marriage by displaying the Moon Rabbit with the full moon in the East part of their home. For those who suspect their spouse is already cheating, you can call on the help of **Kurukulle**, the powerful Goddess of Love. Invoking her presence in your life imbues you with her talent for enchantment, giving you your power back when it comes to your spouse and your marriage. You can display her **Banner of Love** or carry the **Red Tara Home Protection Amulet** – this powerful talisman designed with her image and all her implements of love will repair damage already done to your marriage, while strengthening the bond

Kurukulle's Banner of Love

between you and your spouse. Kurukulle's powers of magnetism will also make it difficult for others to adversely affect your marriage.

We also advise chanting her mantra daily:
OM KURUKULLE HRIH SOHA (21 times or 108 times)

STUDY LUCK IN 2021

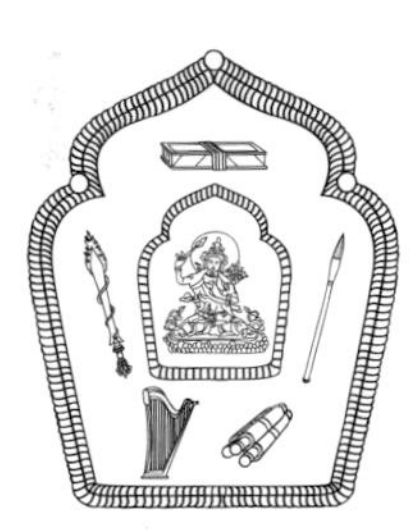

To enhance study luck in 2021, students should call on the help of **Manjushri**, the Buddha of Wisdom. Manjushri with his wisdom sword slices through all ignorance in the mind, enhancing one's wisdom and knowledge. Invoking his help benefits not just students and those studying for exams, but also anyone needing to make important decisions and life choices. He clears the mind to make way for effective and efficient accumulation of knowledge – so that "your knowledge is vast, and your understanding complete". This year we have designed a **Manjushri Home Amulet** for scholars and students to place on their study desk. Manjushri's seed syllable is "DHIH" and chanting this repeatedly in one breath until you run out of breath is the best way to invoke his presence.

You can also chant Manjushri's wisdom mantra:
OM AH RAPA CHA NA DHIH

Make it a habit to chant his mantra either 21 times or 108 times (1 mala) before you sleep each night, or when you can find some quiet time during the day. We suggest you get yourself a **Manjushri Wisdom Mala** which you reserve specially for this purpose – chanting only Manjushri's Wisdom Mantra. This sharpens the mala's power and effectiveness when it comes to study luck, as the energies you direct into the mala as you chant becomes concentrated, making it more and more potent the more you use it.

HEALTH LUCK IN 2021

The Illness Star has flown into the North, the sector of the Rat. This affects all those born in Rat years, but also those whose main doors or bedrooms are located in the North of the home, or those who spend a lot of time in the North sector. Those afflicted with sickness or health problems should have the **Healing Deer** in the North.

Health risks continue to look like a threat going into 2021 so we have designed several potent health and protective talismans to keep everyone safe.

Our **mantra ring** this year features Medicine Buddha's mantra on the outside and Vairocana's mantra on the inside. Medicine Buddha comes to the aid of anyone who is sick and who calls to him for help. Vairocana is the Buddha that protects against contagious diseases.

COVID-19 has been a life-altering phenomenon for the whole world throughout the last year, and as we move into 2021, it does not look like things will revert quite back to normal. We need to continue to practise vigilance following new guidelines as they get discovered to keep safe. Mask up, keep your social distance and get used to a new way of living.

The science of feng shui meanwhile always advocates protection before enhancement, so we strongly advise everyone irrespective of their animal signs to always wear or carry health and protective amulets. It can literally save your life!

The **Medicine Buddha-Vairocana Mantra Ring** is excellent to help keep you safe during these strange times and troubled times.

This year we also strongly recommend the **Health Talisman with Tortoise and Snake**. The Tortoise and Snake are two spiritual creatures associated with longevity, known for their potent powers to heal. The tortoise provides stability both in physical and mental health, while the Snake represents control over the nagas, spirits that can cause ill health and sickness when they are left to their own mischievous devices.

All signs whose element luck tables indicate a poor health category should also place these health cures near to them or carry as portable amulets.

Element Luck of the Sheep in 2021

Chapter 2

- Wood Sheep – 6 & 66 years
- Water Sheep – 18 & 78 years
- Metal Sheep – 30 & 90 years
- Earth Sheep – 42 years
- Fire Sheep – 54 years

ELEMENT LUCK OF THE SHEEP IN 2021

The Sheep's luck takes a dip this year. While your life force ratings are good, your spirit essence is bad and your success luck very bad. This weak element luck showing warns that all Sheep MUST apply element therapy to strengthen your inner and outer energy, or else it will be extremely difficult to achieve any kind of success from the year. One's element luck indicates one's own vitality, no matter what external forces are doing. When your external luck is good, a strong inner essence allows you to capture that luck. But when your external luck is bad, it becomes even more imperative to have a strong inner resolve.

The Sheep sign faces a difficult year with the #3 Quarrelsome Star in its sector. While you have one *Big Auspicious Star* coming from the direction of your astrological secret friend and soulmate the Horse, you have a *Yin House Star* from the direction of the Monkey. You also have the *Sui Po Star* in your sector. All these are indications that it will be far from a smooth-sailing year for those born under the Sheep sign.

Using powerful element placements is a first step to protecting your personal feng shui. To strengthen your spirit essence, you need to increase Earth energy around you. Natural crystals are best, and these serve

ELEMENT LUCK OF

	METAL SHEEP 90/30 years	WATER SHEEP 78/18 years	WOOD SHEEP 66/6 years
Life Force	**good** G	**good** G	**good** G
Health	**good** G	**very good** GG	**excellent** GGG
Wealth	bad x	**excellent** GGG	very bad xx
Success	very bad xx	very bad xx	very bad xx
Spirit Essence	bad x	bad x	bad x

THE SHEEP IN 2021

FIRE SHEEP 54 years	EARTH SHEEP 42 years	2021 Element
good G	**good** G	Earth
very bad xx	**neutral** Gx	Earth 
very good GG	**neutral** Gx	Metal 
very bad xx	very bad xx	Water
bad x	bad x	Fire 

also to strengthen your intrinisic Earth energy. The best are natural crystal balls, as the smooth shape of the balls bring the harmonious energies you need to counter the anger energies emanating from the #3 star. Place such crystals in the SW.

Your personal success luck or *lung ta* can be given a good boost with the **Victorious Windhorse Carrying a Jewel**. Because the Horse has a special astrological connection to your sign, displaying horses is very lucky for the Sheep. You can display horses of all kinds in the home and they will always be lucky for you. This year this is especially the case, as the Horse is the sign which brings you *Big Auspicious* luck.

There is little to help the Sheep from its element Luck indications, thus you must work doubly hard to combat feelings of negativity that may wash over you from time to time. Do not allow yourself to succumb to a downward spiral. Oftentimes, one negative thought leads to another, and then the problem begins, because if left unchecked, such thoughts can lead you to dark places and their growth can become exponential.

As well as from element therapy, the Sheep should carry the **"Om" Dakini Spirit Essence Enhancing Amulet** to fortify inner vigor and confidence. When one is going through a period with low spirit essence, one becomes more susceptible to wandering spirits, negative hexes and even black magic. When your shield is down, which happens when your element luck is weak, dark forces need not even be projected towards you – you can become "collateral damage". For the Sheep this year, we recommend the **"Anti-Black Magic" Medallion** to counter this affliction.

ALL Sheep should carry the **28 Hums Protection Wheel Amulet**. Hum is an extremely powerful seed syallable and depicted with the Dharmachakra Wheel, it propels away all bad vibrations. It will keep you safe from all kinds of harm, including harm that you may bring onto yourself through destructive thoughts or unwise decisions.

Another useful amulet for the Sheep is the **Element Balancing Medallion**. When all elements in your chart are in balance, you can more easily achieve harmony, success and happiness. But this year the Sheep's elements are out of sync, so you need to work at correcting that imbalance.

All Sheep-born in 2021 suffer from weak spirit essence, which needs correction. You can do this by wearing the Element Balancing Medallion and by carrying the "Om" Dakini Spirit Enhancing Amulet.

Some Sheep have better element luck in other categories, so not all Sheep go through the same luck patterns, but ALL Sheep in 2021 need to strengthen their inner resolve.

The Sheep is the great paramour of the Chinese Zodiac. Whether male or female, you possess great talent in using your wiles to get your way with others, who get instantly enthralled by your charm and appeal. While outwardly you may appear soft-spoken, reserved or even bashful, you always know exactly what you are doing. There are few animal signs as good at twisting others around their little fingers as the Sheep. But this year is different, as you lose some of that innate self-confidence. And you need to work at getting it back.

While the Sheep is the master plotter and planner, this year you may not know what it is you are trying to plan or plot. You may find yourself losing your way a little, thus you need to re-anchor yourself and start setting yourself definitive goals. Those with a strong mentor figure in your life will not feel so lost, but others may be left floundering.

This year, do work at being more decisive about what you want. Sometimes it is not the actual decision that counts but simply about whether you have any convictions at all. Pick a stand, then stand by it. Don't allow yourself to sway too easily with the wind. There is nothing wrong in changing your mind, but change it too frequently and others will stop taking you seriously.

WEALTH LUCK FOR THE DIFFERENT SHEEP

Wealth luck differs for the different element Sheep, but especially benefits the **78-year-old** and the **18-year-old Water Sheep** in 2021. These two Sheep enjoy excellent element wealth luck, which suggests that financially you will be secure, and your wealth can grow. The **54-year-old Fire Sheep** also has very good element wealth luck. To take full advantage, these Sheep should display the **Tree Bringing 3 Kinds of Wealth** in your living space; this will add growth energy to your wealth potential, boosting career and investment luck, and for some of you, even attract a windfall.

The **42-year-old Earth Sheep** has neutral element wealth luck, suggesting that while you could be doing better financially, you are not in trouble. Even if cash flow becomes tight, you find a way to cope.

The **30-year-old Metal Sheep** has a less robust indication in the wealth luck category. The advice for this Sheep is to steer clear of risky investments. For you, the best strategy is to maintain a sufficiently diversified portfolio and do not succumb to taking financial risks, no matter how irresistible, as luck is simply not with you when it comes to money matters in 2021.

The **66-year-old Wood Sheep** has its wealth category at a VERY BAD level, so this is a warning to take serious steps to preserve your wealth. Avoid any measure of risk when it comes to money. This is not a year for frivolous expenditures. Unexpected expenses could crop up, disrupting your personal financial plan for the year. Be conservative, do not spend in excess, and limit your exuberance when it comes to spending money. This Sheep benefits from the **"Hum" Dakini Wealth Protection Amulet.**

HEALTH OF THE SHEEP

The only Sheep with anything serious to worry about when it comes to health is the **54-year-old Fire Sheep**. For this Sheep, you should pay more attention to your physical wellbeing. Go for regular check-ups. If you don't feel well for any reason, get it looked at. Do not leave health concerns to a point when it is too late to do anything about it. While you may be active and feeling fit as a fiddle, never take your health for granted, especially this year.

This Sheep should carry **Health Amulets** and have the **Medicine Buddha and 7 Sugatas Gau** near you. Be mindful not to expose yourself to infectious viruses; in this era of pandenics, you must absolutely not take any risks when it comes to contagious diseases. If there are quarantine recommendations in place, follow them! Don't be foolhardy and think you are invincible, because this year, health-wise, you are not.

This is a year when you cannot rely on your element luck to help you. Your Life Force is strong, but your Inner Essence is far from robust. Everything stems from nurturing your self-confidence this year.

Find a way to build up your self-confidence – whether by doing more of the activities that you are good at, mixing with people who build you up, taking a break from stressful engagements, or some other method. For the Sheep in 2021, your mental health becomes a priority, so nurture your soul as well as your bank account.

WOOD SHEEP 6 year old	
life force	good G
health	excellent GGG
wealth	very bad xx
success	very bad xx
spirit essence	bad x

THE 6-YEAR-OLD WOOD SHEEP

Sheep children are gentle souls and tend to be close to their families. While they appear the antithesis of independent, they know exactly what they want and how to get it. Sheep children are generally easy to bring up because they accept authority. They are not naturally rebellious and they try hard to please; but it will always be on their own terms. They know how to wrap both their parents and even all their siblings round their little finger!

They are comfortable when they are "only children" or the youngest child in the family. Their status as baby of the family sits very well on them, as they adore being doted on. They will often look to an authority figure to lean on, and they appreciate an audience for everything they do.

The **6-year-old Sheep** child this year has an exciting time ahead. Most young Sheep will be making the leap from kindergarten to "big school" this year, and they will take this in their stride. In 2021, this little Sheep is in the pink of health with plenty of energy to take on the world. The more they are nurtured and the more attention they get, the better they will do.

You can ensure that your young Sheep child gets the best start in life as they begin their school career by playing the attentive parent. They have no problem with helicopter parenting; in fact they thrive on it!

The best enhancer for this young Sheep is the **Manjushri "Dhih" Scholastic Amulet**. For the Sheep sign, attainments start arriving very early in life. They excel in music and the arts, and when given the right teachers and instruction, they quickly become child prodigies. Far from feeling stifled, they blossom and bloom under guidance and nurture. Put enough focus on your Sheep child and he or she will make you very proud indeed!

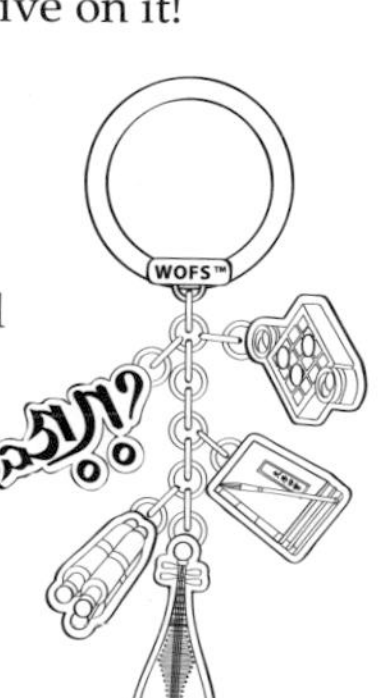

WATER SHEEP 18 year old	
life force	good G
health	very good GG
wealth	excellent GGG
success	very bad xx
spirit essence	bad x

THE 18-YEAR-OLD WATER SHEEP

The Water Sheep is one of the luckiest of the Sheep sign this year. You have excellent wealth luck and very good health luck. Like your Sheep siblings, your spirit essence and success luck need a boost, but you have every other advantage on your side. Most of you will be in your final year of school making plans for College and higher education. Enjoy the time ahead by continuing to work hard. Do not worry too much about actual attainments for now. When you focus on the learning rather than the results, the results will naturally follow.

This Sheep is a naturally hardworking sign, and your advantage will be your great knack for juggling many different things at once. You are good at taking exams because rarely do you get flustered. While you may not outwardly excel through this year, you know when to make it count. This Sheep's big advantage is your natural diplomacy. You attract mentors into your life - teachers and adults in authority who want to see you succeed. Cultivate your relationship with such mentors and they can help you enormously. You can activate this kind of luck by having the **Nobleman Gui Ren Talisman** on your work desk.

This young Sheep will tend to be mature for his or her age, and almost extraordinarily worldly-wise. You take an interest in world affairs and do well in anything to do with humanities. You are an innately empathetic individual with the kindest of hearts, yet you know how to ensure you get your slice of the pie. You're the kind who ends up doing well because you yourself are so generous with your time and your knowledge.

Wealth luck for this Sheep is excellent this year, and some of you will be tempted by opportunities to make money on the side. Some may even be lured into the job market early. You are an incredibly enterprising sign, but don't let the temptation of entrepreneurship undermine your studies. By all means do both, but there is no need to give up one for the other. You can go very far in life so don't let a short-sighted decision limit your choices for the future.

For the young Sheep in 2021, keep your eye on the prize. Clarify your goals. If you stay single-minded about achieving them, you will realize them easily and without fuss.

This Sheep benefits from the **6 Birds Auspicious Multiplier**. This wonderful activator harnesses the power of the Big Auspicious, helping you achieve your most fervent desires. You should also invoke the great **Buddha of Wisdom, Manjushri**. Have his **Gau Home Amulet** in your workspace and carry the **Manjushri "Dhih" Scholastic Amulet** to help you in your studies and guide you in making all the best decisions for your future.

METAL SHEEP 30 year old	
life force	good G
health	good G
wealth	bad x
success	very bad xx
spirit essence	bad x

THE 30-YEAR-OLD METAL SHEEP

The 30-year-old Metal Sheep has good health but bad wealth luck. Your wealth category indicates you must not take risks when it comes to financial decisions. This is not the best of years for the young entrepreneur Sheep.

Making money seems like pulling teeth, and while your efforts reap some results, it will be far from easy-going. When sales are slow, it is easy to get into situations of conflict with those around you. You may take your frustrations out on your workmates, business partners, even your spouse. Don't let a lackluster work year spill over into your personal life and mental well-being.

This is not a year for risking big money. Refrain from taking any kind of financial risks. Even if you have some bright new idea you want to pursue, don't invest too much if you cannot afford to lose it. Financially it will not be an easy year, so the advice is to stay frugal and conservative. Don't overspend. Save the big plans for another time. Wait for the right opportunity to come. Do not become impatient to get going.

Career-wise, this may be a stressful time. You may not be getting along like a house on fire with either your boss or your colleagues. But this is not a good year to change jobs or relocate to another work situation. Better to stay low key and observe as the time is not right for taking action or making significant decisions. When it comes to economic matters, go with the flow. Do not go seeking change, as this is not a year when you can benefit much from initiating change or taking any sort of risks.

Let natural forces decide where and when you need to change course. Refrain from exerting energy unnecessarily. This is not the kind of year to make any kind of life-changing decisions. Better to stay quiet and watchful. In 2021, whatever action you take will simply undermine your energy levels.

For the Metal Sheep this year, going with the flow is better than actively seeking change. Stick with the status quo and enhance what you already have.

This Sheep benefits from carrying wealth amulets to boost money luck. The **Asset Wealth Bull** ensures your wealth can accumulate. It makes sure you don't have to spend everything you earn. For those climbing the career ladder, place the **Nobleman Gui Ren Talisman** on your desk to manifest a mentor figure in your life and bring you the help you need to progress in a steady and professional capacity. It will also make your job far more enjoyable.

EARTH SHEEP 42 year old	
life force	good o
health	neutral ox
wealth	neutral ox
success	very bad xx
spirit essence	bad x

THE 42-YEAR-OLD EARTH SHEEP

A very average year lies ahead for the 42-year-old Earth Sheep. Your element luck is fair but nothing to shout about, making this the kind of year when success will depend on your own efforts. You have neutral health and wealth luck, so the elements bring you neither good nor bad indications. This is no bad thing. What it implies is that this is the kind of year when you can achieve and attain all the goals you set yourself, but first you have to set them, then stay the course.

This year, you do not have the luxury of things simply "falling into your lap". But if you go seeking, you may just then find what you are looking for!

Success luck for this Sheep is weak. You can boost this by having the **Victorious Windhorse Carrying a Jewel** on your workdesk. Do not put too much weight on being lauded and applauded. This is the kind of year when public recognition for your efforts may not be so forthcoming. But your efforts will not go unappreciated by those who matter, even if they may not give voice to it.

Learn to survive on your own praise and approval. The Sheep often needs to feel valued by those around them, as this becomes the fuel that feeds their fire. But in years like this when you face lackluster element luck, it is important to create your own motivation rather than relying on the admiration of others.

In your enthusiasm to breathe life into your work or career, do not neglect your home life. If married and with children, they may need more of your attention than you are currently giving them. Strike a balance in your life.

Work and business will not be a piece of cake but putting in superhuman hours will not change anything. In fact, things may get worse with too much dabbling and overactivity. The words for this Sheep this year are stillness and inactivity. Move quietly and gently, never upsetting the apple cart. Too much bustle and commotion will stir the #3 quarrelsome star into action, which is a whole other problem for the Sheep.

Work at getting along with others, something the Sheep is inherently capable of. Take your mind off the money. This year may not be a landmark year by any measure, but it will be pleasant enough if you play your cards right.

This Sheep benefits from the **6 Birds Auspicious Multiplier**. This will help actualize Big Auspicious for you. You also benefit from wealth amulets and the **Rabbit in the Moon**, to improve relationship luck for you this year. The Rabbit is your astrological ally, and the Moon Rabbit, as well as enhancing for romantic love, improves relationships in all areas of life. Good relationships are the key to success for the Earth Sheep this year.

FIRE SHEEP 54 year old	
life force	good o
health	very bad xx
wealth	**very good** oo
success	very bad xx
spirit essence	bad x

THE 54-YEAR-OLD FIRE SHEEP

The 54-year-old Fire Sheep enjoys very good wealth luck but very bad health luck. For you, this will be a year of balancing your enthusiasm with your well-being. Of all the Sheep, the Fire Sheep is the most courageous and the most outgoing. You are vivacious and spirited, always the life of the party. You win others over with your extremely magnetic charm, which you have by the spadeful.

This year however, relationship luck becomes pricklier as you come under the influence of the #3 quarrelsome star. This is not something you are used to, but you are better equipped than your Sheep siblings to handle the cantankerous energies brought by this troublesome star. "*Stay calm and keep going*" should be your mantra for the year.

Your promising wealth element luck suggests that this could be a year when you benefit from some significantly special developments taking place. This is a year when everything goes well, and you enjoy a good level of professional as well as personal satisfaction.

You take pride in the admiration of peers, and this motivates you to overcome whatever lack of energy you may be feeling. The Sheep has the *Yin House Star* to contend with, and a very weak success indication, but despite the challenges you face, for you, there is money to be made. While accolades and recognition may be harder to come by, when financial matters are under control, these become less important to you. You are secure in your own skin and do not need the commendation of others to prove your self-worth.

Your health however could take better looking after, so do not ignore the physical aspects of your well-being. Remember to exercise, mix up work with play, have enough time for your own relaxation, and watch your diet doesn't become too unhealthy.

For this Sheep, we recommend wearing the **Medicine Buddha-Vairocana Mantra Ring** or carrying the **Medicine Buddha Mantra Wand**. Medicine Buddha provides the ultimate antidote to the removal of success and health obstacles and coming under his protection will ensure the year unfolds happily and successfully for the Fire Sheep.

You should also carry the **Health Talisman Holder with Health Mantras** as you don't want to leave your health to chance. Go for regular checkups and don't ignore warning signals. If you do not feel well, do get it checked out.

WOOD SHEEP 66 year old	
life force	good o
health	excellent ooo
wealth	very bad xx
success	very bad xx
spirit essence	bad x

THE 66-YEAR-OLD WOOD SHEEP

The 66-year-old Wood Sheep benefits from excellent good health this year, but wealth luck is very bad. Here we see two extremes in terms of your health and wealth luck. At this stage of your life, these readings are not necessarily a challenge, as having excellent health luck is more than a blessing. It suggests that physically you are strong and mentally you are in good shape. This means you have the capacity to enjoy life, to travel and be very active in terms of pursuing outdoor interests. You can be as lively as you wish and pursue whatever challenge takes your fancy. Many would describe this as being very blessed indeed, as it means you are unlikely to be suffering any kind of aches and pains, or be threatened with any serious physical condition. Those who might be ill will feel better this year.

It is however necessary to advise those still "investing" or playing the stock markets to go easy and if possible, to refrain from being too active as an investor. This is a year when you must strenuously avoid taking financial risks. If you are exposed to the markets, you are likely to lose money this year. Likewise, it is a good

idea to avoid gambling, as pitting yourself against the luck stakes can get you into trouble. Those still active running their commercial businesses should also refrain from taking risks in their business decisions.

It is true to say that irrespective of how certain you may feel about your money luck, you cannot ignore what the element charts are telling you, which is that your wealth luck is very low this year. Better to play safe and refrain from making any significant financial decisions.

This Sheep should boost asset wealth luck with **Wealth Cabinets**. These will ensure your wealth continues to grow so you have enough should you reach a time when you want to retire or spend on a rainy day. You should also carry the **Good Fortune Lock Amulet** to protect against losing money this money. For those still actively playing the stock market, display the **Winning Chip Talisman** to get speculative luck on your side.

WATER SHEEP 78 year old	
life force	good G
health	very good GG
wealth	excellent GGG
success	very bad xx
spirit essence	bad x

THE 78-YEAR-OLD WATER SHEEP

The 78-year-old Water Sheep enjoys very good heath luck and excellent wealth luck. Your spirit essence is weak, so you may find it difficult to get motivated and you may catch yourself feeling listless and lacking energy. This will not be the most inspired of years for this Sheep unless you can find a new passion to get excited about. But at your age, you should be taking things easy and not allow yourself to worry too much about work-related matters.

Enjoy the year. Be thankful your health is in a good place. You would have experienced life to a huge extent already, so do let go of mundane worries. Spend more time with family and take pleasure in your grandkids. If you still have the physical ability to do so, continue with your active lifestyle. Take joy in your loved ones and in nurturing your descendants. They are amongst the best of life's blessings.

is obviously missing Fire, the element that indicates WEALTH LUCK, so the year lacks opportunities to make money.

However, the eight characters in the Four Pillars – made up of 4 heavenly stems and 4 earthly branches – are not the only elements present. The interaction of these elements, depending on where and how they are positioned within the chart, generates a set of hidden elements as well as special stars. We use this chapter to analyse each part of this year's Four Pillars chart, and mention the most significant findings.

2021's Paht Chee chart indicates a strong self-element of Water, which boosts competitive energies and puts everyone on edge. Friends become foes when the stakes are raised, so this is a year to constantly watch one's back. The year's chart is unbalanced; it is missing the vital element of FIRE, which represents wealth and financial success. It is thus a year when it will be difficult to make much headway in the creation of new wealth. Profits may take a long time to get realized and there are few speculative gains to be made.

Prosperity comes with hard work rather than with a stroke of luck. This is definitely not a year to strike it rich via the lottery.

Here is a closer look at the most important indications this year:

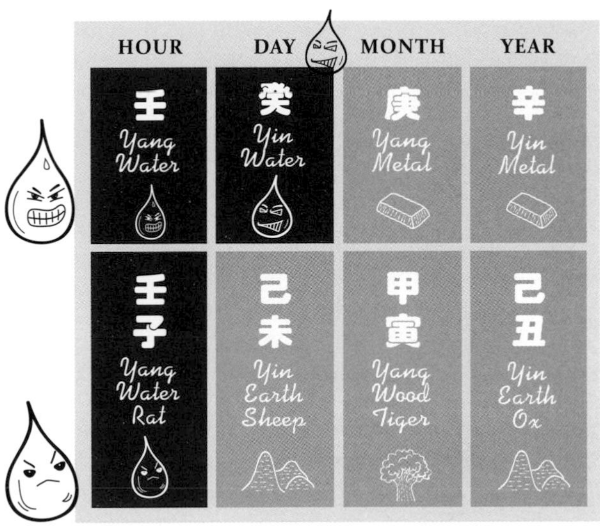

There appears to be way too much Water in this year's chart.

A YEAR OF STRONG WATER indicating a competitive year

First, the self-element of the year is Strong Water. It is a year when rivalry becomes enhanced and when politics can get unscrupulous. Watch your back and reserve your trust for your very innermost circle. Indeed, even your inner circle could let you down if the circumstances dictate. Betrayals happen of their own accord, sometimes without the guilty party's conscious intention. Learn to forgive and move on but protect yourself by being more careful and by putting safeguards in place. Remove temptation where you can and stay close to all you are working with.

PROTECTION: Those in business are advised to carry the **Kuan Kung Anti-Betrayal Amulet**. This will protect you against the betrayal of others and being let down by people whom you trust. It keeps you prepared for whatever the winds and waters bring your way.

In any competitive endeavour, it could well feel like a fight to the death. Diplomatic compromises will be difficult to achieve, and different factions and interest groups find it harder to reach win-win scenarios. But it is nevertheless important to try. Sometimes being the bigger person will help; but recognize when you have to fight and when you don't. Indeed, do not mistakenly think you are in fact being the magnanimous one when you are being taken for a fool. It is a year when it is prudent to carry protection always. The **28 Hums Protection Amulet** is an excellent all-round amulet that will safeguard you from all kinds of harm.

SOLUTION: The excess of Water energy in the chart needs to be resolved. Use **WOOD energy** to weaken the excess Water. Having plenty of greenery and live plants in your living space will help re-balance the energies and will also bring vital growth energy to a year which lacks the presence of the *Lap Chun*, or "Spring".

This year, having plenty of plants and Wood energy around you will help soak up the excess Water in the year's chart.

BALANCE OF YIN & YANG

Second, there are two Yang pillars and two Yin Pillars. There is thus a good mix between energetic periods and restive ones, with no dominance of work over play, or vice versa. The Yang Month and Hour Pillars bring great vitality, while the Yin Year and Day Pillars bring balance. There should be more than enough strength to propel positive chi forward and upward. People in general are open to different viewpoints. If negative energies can be kept under control and sufficiently subdued, the year is then able to propel forward, benefitting many.

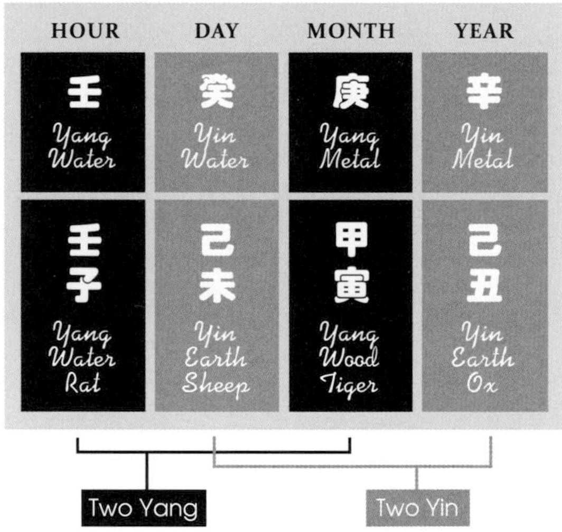

This year there is good balance between Yang and Yin in the year's Four Pillars chart.

CLASH OF SHEEP WITH OX

indicating strong conflict energy

Third, there is a clash of SHEEP with OX in the Earth Branches. This clash between two Earth animals suggests that the clash will be between leaders. Earth is the element that represents leadership and rank, thus animosity will likely be between those who are in charge. But because those in power are especially strong this year, fighting can become ferocious, with the damage dealt far-reaching. There will be strong clashes between the leaders of nations.

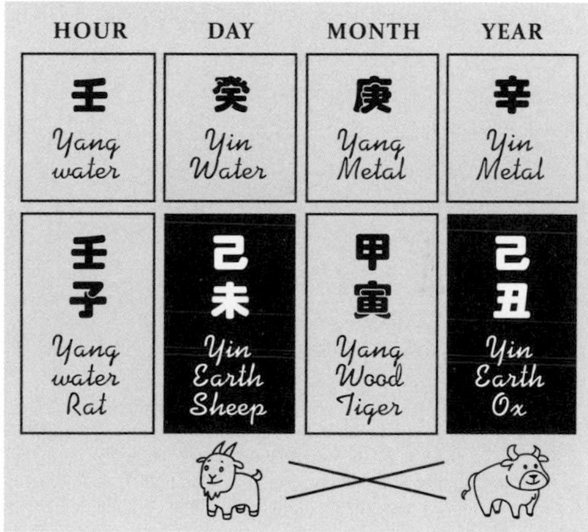

The clash between Ox and Sheep brings many problems to the year, especially between those who are in charge and everyone else, who could end up as collateral damage.

Within family units, because the clash Occurs in the Day Pillar, there is likely to be strong conflict between spouses.

SOLUTION: There may be more marital problems in 2021 with the Sheep in the Self-Spouse pillar clashing with the Year pillar. In the family unit, this coupled with the presence of the *External Flower of Romance* star brings all kinds of problems to husband and wife. Every home this year should have the **"Rabbit in the Moon" Love Enhancer** and better still if both husband and wife carry the **Enhancing Relationships Amulet**. Recognize when an outsider is trying to make trouble in your marriage, and refrain from siding with a third party over your spouse, no matter how much your husband or wife may be annoying you. When you allow an outsider into the mix, this year, such troubles can escalate very quickly.

Enhancing Relationships Amulet

SPECIAL LINK BETWEEN RAT & OX

bringing creativity and inventiveness

Fourth, there is however a very strong affinity between RAT and OX in the Earthly Branches of the Year and Hour Pillar. This is a heaven sent because it serves to repair some of the damage resulting from the Ox-Sheep clash. The Year Pillar of the Ox forms a soulmate pairing with the Hour Pillar of the Rat, which means there is a good beginning and a good ending to the year, what the Chinese refer to as having a head and tail, a suggestion that things that

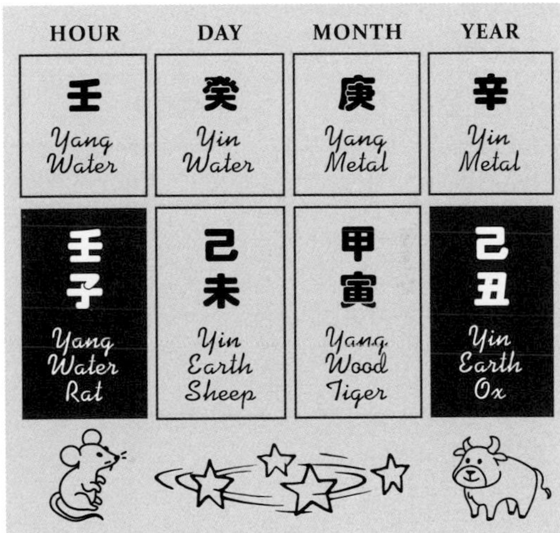

The Rat and Ox in this year's chart form a very special affinity, bringing relationship and completion luck.

get started have a good chance to reach satisfactory completion. The two signs of Rat and Ox are extremely harmonious together, generating the *House of Cleverness and Creativity*, with the Rat starting and the Ox completing. This endows the year with wonderful ingenuity and inventiveness.

> The presence of the Rat & Ox in the year's Four Pillars suggests a year when true friendship means something.

These two signs are also a secret-friend pair, indicating **good friendship luck** through the year. While there are indications of strong competition and rivalry, there is also much potential for firm friendships, and opportunities for friends to demonstrate their loyalties and allegiance. A year perhaps of finding out who one's true friends are.

ENHANCER: Get the **"Perfect Partnerships to Attract Big Wealth" Enhancer**. This enhancer featuring the Ox and Rat will boost all the positive indications of this combination. Display in a prominent area in the home; in the living room, or near the dining room where you spend a lot of time. The number "8" on the Ox activates for the missing wealth luck of the year.

NO PROSPERITY LUCK INDICATED

... but there is hidden wealth

Fifth, there is MISSING WEALTH. Fire which represents wealth is completely missing from the main chart. What this indicates is that it will be difficult to make money. New businesses will take time getting off the ground, sales will be slow, industries that are shrinking will continue to do so, while their replacements will take time to take flight. Profit margins get squeezed as information becomes more and more freely available, and technology continues to disrupt at breakneck pace. This year, if one wants to stay afloat, it is vitally important to keep up with the world that is so rapidly changing around us.

While there will be results and completions, it will nevertheless feel like an interim year, because we are at the beginning end of a new cycle, and not quite at the close of the current period. 2021 represents the second animal sign of the cycle after the new decade last year opened with the Rat, and we are heading towards the end of Period 8, and the beginning of Period 9, but we are not quite there yet.

There is a lack of obvious wealth in 2021, but those who look harder can find gold. This year, there is HIDDEN WEALTH brought by the sign of the TIGER.

Before the New Year arrives, make sure you get our specially created **Red Wealth Wallet** featuring the Wealth Ox. It is auspicious each year to change to a new wallet and especially lucky to take some money from your old wallet and transfer it over to your new wallet. Doing so for this year will ensure you take some of the energy of last year, and carry it over into the following year. In 2021 you definitely want to do this, as the previous Year of the Rat carried two *Lap Chuns*, or two "Springs" while this year has none.

Keep the lights in your home brightly turned on throughout the year, especially in the WEST sector, which plays host to the Prosperity Star #8.

POWERFUL SPIRITUAL ENHANCER: For Wealth Luck that is potent and long-lasting, an excellent ritual to incorporate into your life is the **White Dzambala Ritual**. Invite in **White Dzambala and the Four Dakinis** who pull in

wealth from the four directions. Display in a respectful place in the home and recite White Dzambala's mantra as regularly as you can.

White Dzambala's Mantra:
Om Padma Krodha Arya Dzambala
Hridaya Hum Phat

When you gaze upon him and chant his mantra regularly, he manifests great riches in your life and attracts incredible opportunities that can bring wealth of a big meaningful and lasting kind.

INVITE IN THE ROOSTER: The Rooster brings the #8 Wealth Star in 2021, so it is extremely auspicious to have many images of Roosters in the home this year. The Rooster is also the symbol that ensures politicking is kept to a minimum, protecting against harmful gossip and slander. The Rooster is also wonderful for protecting the marriage, preventing any troublesome third party from trying to come between husband and wife.

Rooster
with Crown

with the Ox sign of the year, a reminder that those who retain their passion for success will benefit from its presence. This star suggests there is nothing that cannot be achieved for those prepared to work hard. The more ambitious one is, the further one can go this year.

STAR OF PROSPECTS: To activate this star in your favour, keep an **image of an Ox** near you. We suggest the **Bejewelled Asset Bull** to magnify wealth luck and to ensure the hard work you put in meets with proportionate success. This bull has been designed with an auspicious saddle in red, the colour that signifies wealth in 2021, wearing a harness of coins and stepping on a pile of wealth and ingots, symbolizing the accumulation of assets.

This beautiful enhancer will allow you to accumulate everything you work for and ensure you do not spend everything you earn. It will also increase the opportunities that come your way.

THE STAR OF POWERFUL MENTORS

brings Benefactor Luck

The Star of Powerful Mentors which was also in last year's chart makes another appearance in 2021. This star is brought by the OX in the Year Pillar and the Heavenly Stem of YANG METAL in the Month Pillar. This star is especially beneficial for the younger generation, who have the auspicious luck of influential people turning up in their lives to help them, giving them meaningful advice and powerful support.

HOUR	DAY	MONTH	YEAR
壬 Yang Water	癸 Yin Water	庚 Yang Metal	辛 Yin Metal
壬 子 Yang Water Rat	己 未 Yin Earth Sheep	甲 寅 Yang Wood Tiger	己 丑 Yin Earth Ox

The Star of Powerful Mentors is particularly beneficial for the younger generation.

intense aggression. It indicates the strengthening of the underdog's chi, so it points to a rise of revolutionary fervour, people revolting against authority. Strikes continue, spawning groups around the globe to walk similar paths. Protests advocating for greater equality, non-discrimination, fighting against police brutality and other social injustices continue to pick up steam. There will be anger, passion, rioting and violence.

At its pinnacle, the presence of this star suggests the emergence of powerful leaders on opposing sides, or of highly influential opposition to established leaders. It suggests the rise of a people who seize power by fair means or foul. The name of this star is ***Yang Ren,*** which describes ***"yang essence sharp blade that inflicts damage"***. This is a star with great potential for either very good or very bad influences to materialize during the year, although generally, the influence tends to be more negative than positive. There is risk of revolution and of the toppling of unpopular leaders in power.

The Aggressive Sword Star brings potential for violence & bloodshed. This star must be strongly subdued.

In this year's chart, the *Star of Aggressive Sword* is created by the strong YIN WATER of the DAY pillar, with the presence of the OX in the YEAR pillar. Here, note that the WATER element is strong in the chart, making the presence of the Aggressive Sword much more negative. It indicates that those emerging as leaders for the underdog in 2021 will end up being heavy-handed and quick-tempered. They may be charismatic but they will also be strong-willed, conceited, arrogant, overbearing and self-centered - all nasty traits that spell the potential for bloodshed and violence wherever they emerge. There is real danger of this this year!

CURE: To shield against the harmful effects of the Aggressive Sword Star, the best remedy is a powerful spiritual Stupa. The **Kumbum Stupa** is especially beneficial as it contains one hundred holy images, invoking the protection of all the world's Wisdom Protectors. This Stupa will ensure that all family members living within the home stay protected against aggression or violence of any kind. It is also a good idea to wear or carry the **28 Hums Protection Wheel Amulet** at all times.

Kumbum Stupa

THE FLOWER OF ROMANCE STAR (EXTERNAL) *makes marriages vulnerable*

This star is sometimes confused with the *Peach Blossom Star* because it addresses the destiny of love; but while both influence love and romance, they are very different in their effects. When the Flower of Romance is present, it suggests love blossoms easily, but it is not the kind of love that leads to marriage and family. It indicates instead the possibility of extramarital affairs, bringing stress and unhappiness to married couples. There is also a difference between ***internal*** and ***external romance***, and in this year of the Ox, it is unfortunately the latter that prevails. So the year

HOUR	DAY	MONTH	YEAR
壬 Yang Water	癸 Yin Water	庚 Yang Metal	辛 Yin Metal
壬 子 Yang Water Rat	己 未 Yin Earth Sheep	甲 寅 Yang Wood Tiger	己 丑 Yin Earth Ox

The External Flower of Romance Star brings stress and risk of infidelity to marriages.

is likely to see increased occurrences of infidelity and break-ups of marriages.

Marriages are vulnerable to the External Flower of Romance this year.

The SHEEP in the Day Pillar and RAT of the Hour Pillar indicate the presence of the *External Romance Star*, making all marriages vulnerable to straying by husband OR wife. Things are made worse as the Sheep clashes with the ruling animal of the year, the Ox. This causes misunderstandings between couples, and danger of an outsider fanning the flames from the side.

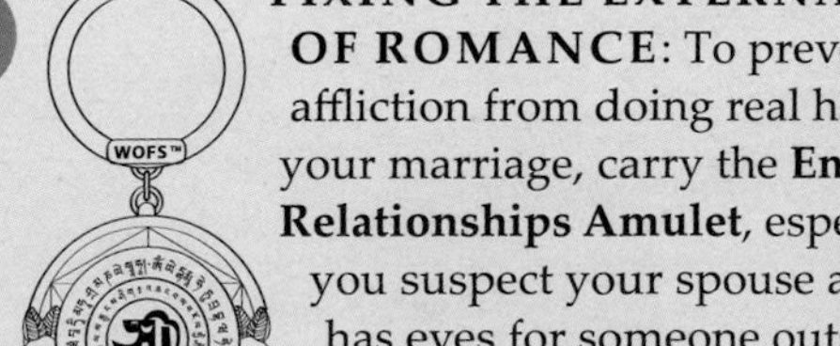

FIXING THE EXTERNAL STAR OF ROMANCE: To prevent this affliction from doing real harm to your marriage, carry the **Enhancing Relationships Amulet**, especially if you suspect your spouse already has eyes for someone outside your marriage. Or if you are constantly fighting with each other, or forced into a situation when you have to spend large amounts of time apart (e.g. if one of you commutes to a different country for work, or travel a lot for work). It is also a good idea to display a pair of **Marriage Happiness Ducks** in the SW of the home, or if you suspect something

of the home where the star is located is kept well-energized and active throughout the year.

In 2021, it benefits to keep the center of the home very active! Have friends over & use this space well.

Rearrange your furniture so you naturally gravitate to the center of your home. The more you include this space in daily usage, the better the luck of the whole family for this coming year.

2021's chart suits homes with open plan layouts arranged around the center part of the home. This is where the luck of auspicious heaven energy congregates this year, and keeping this part of the home lively and vibrant with lots of music, chatter and activity will serve to "activate" this star, bringing it to life!

Work at repositioning your furniture and seating if you have to. This year it is extremely auspicious for all members of the household to spend plenty of time in the center sector, and when you have guests, entertain them in this part of the home. If your home has a piano, place it in the center so every time someone sits down to play it, the sector gets energized.

If your home is not an open-concept one, keep the doors to the center room in the home ajar as much as possible.

You want the energy that emanates from the center to seep into all other areas of the home. The more you energize this part of your house, and the more you suppress the bad luck sectors, the better the luck of the whole household for the year.

ENHANCE THE CENTER GRID
with the Celestial Water Dragon

This year, every household benefits from the presence of the **Celestial Water Dragon**. Place this celestial creature in the center of your home and of your office. The celestial Dragon is the ultimate symbol of good fortune and its deep blue colour and cloud imagery suggest its heavenly origins. This Dragon is auspicious wherever he is displayed, but this year he especially benefits the center part of the home, which houses the Heaven Star #6.

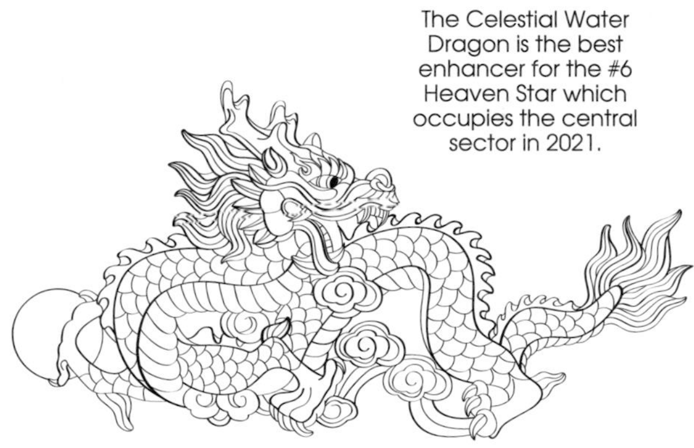

The Celestial Water Dragon is the best enhancer for the #6 Heaven Star which occupies the central sector in 2021.

Placing the Celestial Water Dragon here will attract plenty of new and lucrative opportunities into your life, as well as the patrons, mentors and contacts you need to support you in whatever path you choose to take. Individuals and organizations who are in a position to help you and to open doors for you, will somehow find their way into your life. The presence of the celestial Dragon always attracts abundance and success, and this year, inviting in this Dragon brings a very special kind of good fortune indeed.

Invoking the power of THE EIGHT IMMORTALS

Another excellent energizer for the center is the **8 Celestial Immortals Plaque**. The 8 Immortals bring eight kinds of good fortune and protects against harm. In Chinese mythology, they are a revered group of legendary beings each with a unique talent or ability.

Place the 8 Immortals Plaque in the center of the home in 2021.

These eight saints have been depicted in Chinese art since time immemorial as they are believed to bestow wealth, longevity and spiritual awakening on all who glance upon them.

Depicted as a group, they bring a balanced basket of good fortune and protection for the whole family. They hail from the 8 different compass directions and are usually shown with their unique symbols representing the luck each brings.

Zhang Guo Lao, protector of the North, **brings the luck of good descendants**. His symbol is the bamboo flute and his element is Water. He enjoys drinking wine and is famous for making his own which had curative and healing powers. He is said to be able to drink poison without harm and offers protection against the dark arts. He is often shown with his companion, the mule.

Chao Guo Jiu, protector of the Northeast, **brings the luck of control**. He is excellent for those in positions of authority who have to motivate and retain the support of those they command. His element is Earth and his symbol are the castanets. According to legend, he went to great lengths to avoid casualties of war, protecting the innocent from harm during battle. He is skilled in the magical arts and possesses great wisdom and charisma to lead with great authority.

Lee Dong Bin, protector of the West, **brings protection against evil**. His element is Metal and his implement is the Magic Sword. He is famed for being a great scholar and poet, and for his exceptional intelligence. While he had certain character flaws – he was a serial womanizer - he was known for his dedication to helping others elevate their spiritual growth.

He Xian Gu, protector of the Southwest, **bestows family and marriage luck**. Her element is Earth and her symbol is the Lotus Blossom. The only lady among the 8, she has also grown to become a symbol of woman power. She is often accompanied by a mythical bird said to reign over all birds, bringing new opportunities from near and far. She helps stabilize married couples, protecting the sacred sanctity of marriage and bestowing a happy family life. She protects against troublemakers who threaten to break up happy families. For those who are single, she is said to attract marriage opportunities and suitable suitors.

Han Xiang Zi, protector of the Southeast, **brings healing energies** to those who are sick, but more particularly, he helps heal those with a broken heart. His element is Wood and his symbol is the flute. His legendary past involves the tragic love story where he fell in love with the daughter of the Dragon King, who did not grant the couple his blessings. Theirs was a star-crossed romance without a happy ending, but the bamboo flute he wields was said to be a gift from his beloved. Playing on his flute healed him emotionally, and from there on he vowed to help others the same way.

Lan Chai He, protector of the Northwest, **brings scholastic and creative luck**. His element is Metal and his symbol the flower basket. He is often shown with his swan, symbolic of his lyrical gifts. He is said to have become immortal when the Monkey King bestowed 500 years of magic upon him. His companion is the Monkey. As well as his flair for the arts, he is said to possess a sharp intelligence and wit.

The powerful Fire star #9 brings vitality to all who come under its influence, and its presence in the ruling animal sector bodes well for the coming year. This star benefits homes that face NE, and individuals whose bedrooms or office rooms are located NE, as well as those born under the signs of Ox and Tiger.

The #9 in the NE suggests that the central #6 heavenly star gets strengthened. This is a lucky star for most of the year, except for months when monthly flying stars here are unfavourable – i.e. March, May, July, August and December 2021. When unfavourable monthly stars visit, ensure you have the relevant cures in place and keep this sector less active during these times.

ENHANCERS FOR THE NORTHEAST

The NE benefits from the **9 Golden Dragons Plaque** featuring nine celestial Dragons that bestow power and generates the capacity to pursue all one's grandest ambitions conviction and courage.

Having nine Dragons in the NE allows you to stay focused on long-term goals without getting distracted,

Display the 9 Golden Dragons Plaque in the NE.

or discouraged by short-term difficulties. They protect you against those who wish to see you fail, and shields you from the effects of less ambitious relatives or acquaintances who do not have your vision.

Displaying this plaque in the NE of your home or office ensures you have the support of not one but *nine* Dragons, the number that symbolizes completion and abundance. The number 9 is a magical number as it is a number that always reduces back to itself when multiplied. It also strengthens the #9 star, which is getting stronger as we move rapidly towards a fast-approaching Period of 9.

BUILD YOUR WEALTH: You should also activate the NE with a collection of **Wealth Cabinets**. These wealth cabinets symbolize an accumulation of asset wealth, meaning that the money you make accrues into ever-larger amounts that can last into the many generations. Energizing the NE helps you to make enough money so you do not have to spend everything you earn. It allows you to grow wealthy enough to carve out a secure, comfortable and worry-free future for yourself and your loved ones.

a love relationship. Invoking the blessings of the **Rabbit in the Moon** ensures that only the positive aspects of love materialize. It will also protect against unpleasantness associated with matters of the heart. They say there is nothing sweeter than love, but they also say that nothing breaks like a heart – remember the song by Mark Ronson and Miley Cyrus? Heartache and heartbreak can be far more painful than physical pain; the #4 in the East brings the Moon Rabbit to life and provides a solution for those looking for happiness in love.

ATTRACTING MARRIAGE OPPORTUNITIES

For those looking for a soul mate, someone you can settle down with and make a future with, or if you are already dating but your partner seems a long way off from proposing marriage, you can speed things along with the help of your **Peach Blossom Animal**. Our new Peach Blossom animals the **Rat**, **Rabbit**, **Horse** and **Rooster** come with trees of fortune enhanced with potent symbols of love and marriage. The **Peach Blossom Rat** brings love and marriage opportunities to the **Sheep**, **Boar** and **Rabbit**. If you are a Sheep looking for love that leads to marriage, or you would like your current partner to propose, display a **Peach Blossom Rat** in the NORTH, or in the EAST in 2021.

Peach Blossom Rat

For students, *activate the Scholastic Star in the EAST*

For young people and anyone pursuing their studies, engaged in research or in search of new knowledge, they can activate the scholastic star of the year which flies to the East in 2021. The #4 is also the star number that brings study and exam luck; when properly activated, it has the power to help you achieve success in anything related to scholastic accolades. Enhancing this star improves clarity of mind, allowing you to absorb new knowledge and to process it with much greater efficiency. Anything requiring cognitive

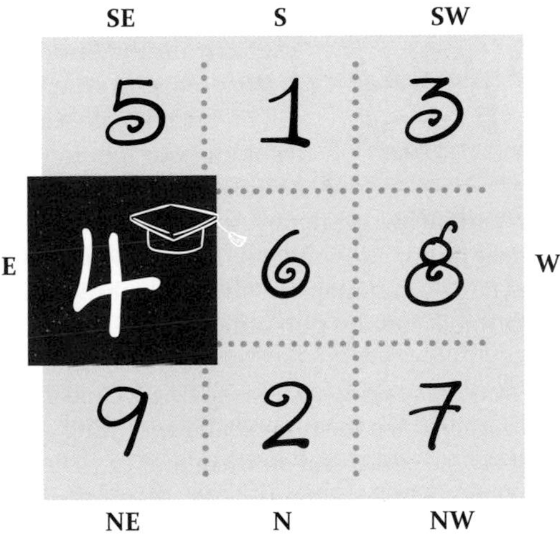

The #4 star in the East is also the Star of Scholarship

The academic path of today is filled with potholes and pitfalls, far more than in the old days, as everything has become so much more competitive. More and more young people are fighting for fewer places at the top universities and colleges; at school, children are faced with competition from classmates with Tiger parents in the sidelines egging them on. For a young mind, it can all become too much, and with all the expectations heaped on young shoulders these days, sometimes all it takes is one bad test or one bad result to cause a child to throw in the towel and just give up.

As parents, we need to imbue in our children not just the impetus to keep striving for the top, but help them understand there will be bumps and disappointments along the way. It is not necessary to perform every single day of the year, to come out top in every single test; what is important is to peak when it counts. The **Dragon Carp** stabilizes one's mind, helping a child along the academic path and to navigate all that comes his or her way with a strong and mature mind, resulting in success when it truly matters.

Transform Five Yellow Misfortune Star *in the Southeast*

The bogus star, the Five Yellow, makes its way into the Southeast this year. The good news is that because the Southeast is a Wood Sector, it mitigates the extent of damage of this dangerous Earth star, as Wood destroys Earth in the cycle of elements. When the Five Yellow flies into a Wood sector, misfortune can be turned into opportunity. This is why we have designed this year's **Five Element Pagoda with a Tree of Life**. This alters the effects of the *wu wang*, suppressing the darker side of this star while

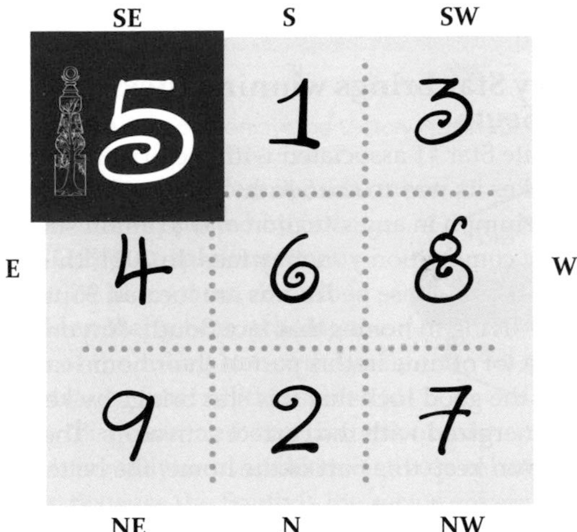

The 5 Yellow afflicts the SE in 2021 but with the correct cure, this Five Yellow has the potential to bring great good luck!

ACTIVATE THE VICTORY STAR:
The best enhancer for the Victory Star is the **Victorious Windhorse Carrying a Jewel**. The Windhorse is the very essence of success luck, known as the magical steed of the folk hero King Gesar, who when riding his Windhorse could never be defeated. His horse with flaming red coat has become synonymous with success and victory, and his image is what is needed whenever one needs to boost one's chances against others in any kind of competitive situation. In 2021, we recommend for everyone to place the Victorious Windhorse in the South. This sector is also the home sector of the Horse, an auspicious creature that emanates pure Fire energy. Displaying images and figurines of horses in the South is thus very appropriate and auspicious indeed.

Activate the #1 Star in the South with the Victorious Windhorse.

BOOST POWER AND AUTHORITY:
For those in positions of leadership and management, the best way to enhance your effectiveness as a leader is with the help of the **Ru Yi**. The Ru Yi is the royal scepter of power, which bestows "the right to rule". In ancient China, anyone in any kind of power would never be seen without a Ru Yi at his side. You can place your Ru Yi in front of you on your work desk, or carry in your bag.

The **Crimson Red Ru Yi with Bats** brings the luck of **success and abundance**. Any boss, head or leader can use the help of this Ru Yi to ensure things between all in their group stay harmonious, joyful and productive at all times. It attracts the luck of abundance and success, so whatever is pursued turns out fruitful and effective. It helps you to ensure all your final goals are reached in the most harmonious way.

Anyone in any kind of leadership position needs a Ru Yi.

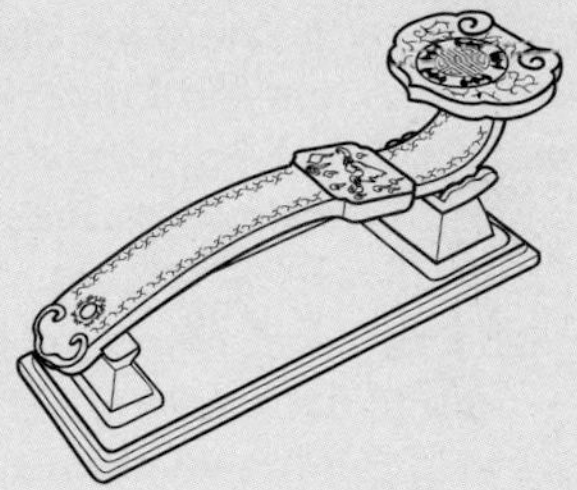

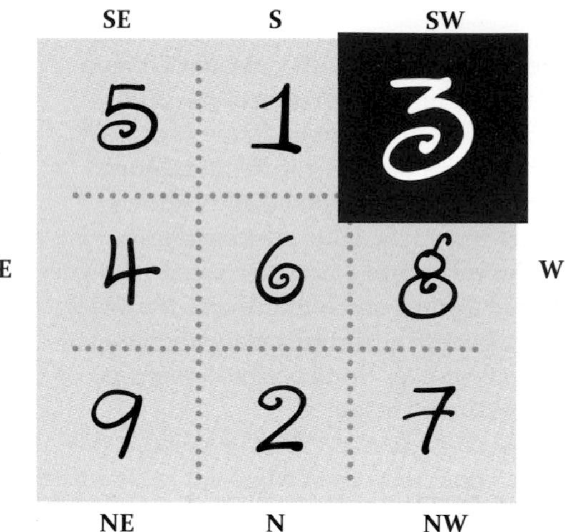

Beware the #3 quarrelsome star in the SW this year.

as the intrinsic Wood energy of the star dominates the Earth energy of the SW. The effects of this star are made worse as the SW also plays host to the **Yin House** from the 24 Mountains. All this suggests that this affliction MUST be taken seriously.

Anything that suggests Fire is an effective cure, so keeping the lights turned on brightly in this sector will help combat the negative energies of this star. **The colour red** is also suitable, so red curtains, rugs and cushion covers here will help very much indeed.

CURES FOR THE QUARRELSOME STAR:
For 2021, the best remedy for the Quarrelsome Star in the SW is the **Nine Phoenix Plaque** in red and gold. These celestial birds in red and gold - which represent the elements of Fire and Metal - work to subdue this troublesome Wood Star. The Fire energy engulfs the Wood of the #3, while the Metal energy of the gold effectively subdues it.

The Nine Phoenix Plaque is an excellent cure against the #3 Quarrelsome Star.

We also recommend placing **red carpets** in this sector, or in the SW portion of any room you spend a lot of time in. Another effective cure for the #3 are the **Red Peace and Harmony Apples**. In Chinese, the word for peaceful is *Ping*, which sounds like the word for apple – *Ping Kor*. This year's Peace Apples comes embossed with the English word "Peace" and the Chinese rhyming couplet carrying the meaning "If your intentions are good and your heart is pure, the world will be peaceful."

Place this pair of apples in the SW to ensure all members of the household stay supportive of one another, and to prevent clashes and conflict from arising. Also an excellent cure for use within the office to maintain a productive and supportive environment between colleagues and workmates.

Enhance Prosperity Star 8 *in the West*

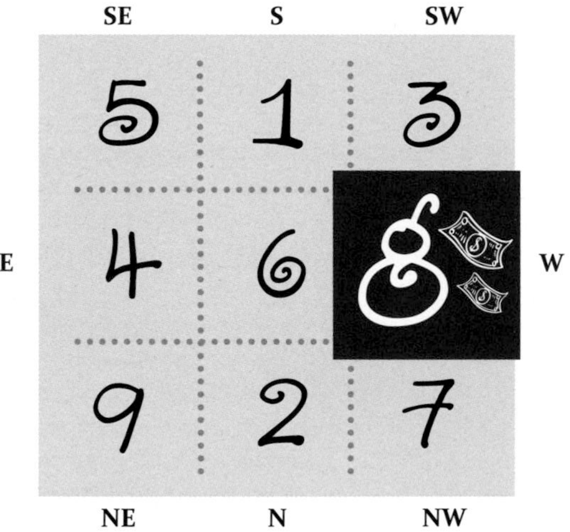

The Wealth Star #8 flies to the West this year.

The very lucky Wealth Star #8 makes its way to the West, the sector of the Rooster. This star is also known as the *Current Prosperity Star*, as we are currently in the Period of 8. The West is the sector that represents children and descendants, suggesting that the wealth this sector brings will last into the long term, reaching future generations and for many generations to come. It points to a successful accumulation of assets over time if properly energized.

In 2021, the West can be considered one of the luckiest areas of the home, because it enjoys this auspicious #8 star. The strong energy of the current period emanating from this sector benefits all homes whose main entrances face West, and all bedrooms and offices located in the West benefit from this luck. The West is also the place of the youngest daughter, so the wealth this sector brings benefits the young girls of the house.

WEALTH luck takes root in the WEST sector this year, so this is the area of the home you should enhance for greater prosperity luck.

Remember that to activate the luck of this auspicious star #8, the West should be thoroughly imbued with yang energy - this means lots of activity, lots of noise and plenty of bright lights. When there is movement, sound, chatter and merry-making, the number 8 comes to life, bringing good fortune and big prosperity. In the constellations, 8 is a "man-made star" with two assistants – on the right and on the left - so that at its strongest moments, it brings wealth and great nobility.

When the 8 can turn dangerous...

Beware however. The number becomes negative when afflicted by structures in the environment that threaten its location. If the West sector of your home has too much Metal energy, or if there are harmful physical structures that cause poison arrows to direct threatening energy your way, that is when the number 8 can bring harm to young children especially young daughters of the household, causing illness to arise. If there are such structures external to your home, but towards the West, it is important to block the view with curtains, or dissipate the killing energy with **facetted crystal balls**. These will disperse the worst of the killing breath before it has the chance to enter your home.

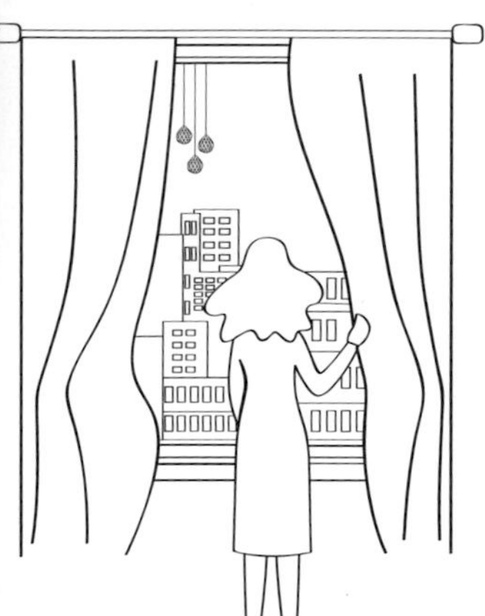

If the view from your window to the WEST is of a threatening looking building with sharp edges or poison arrows, keep the curtains in this area closed to block the offending view from spoiling your feng shui. Hang facetted crystal balls here.

ACTIVATE FOR WEALTH IN THE WEST

The best way to manifest wealth luck in 2021 is the make sure the West part of your home is well-energized with wealth symbols. Because this is the year of the Ox, this creature is especially lucky as it symbolizes harnessing the good fortune of the year. Because the West represents children and descendants, this prosperity luck benefits the whole family not just in the present but into the long term.

The Ox has great power to attract abundant good fortune in 2021. Displaying images of the Ox in all sizes and permutations is thus so lucky this year! For the collectors among you, a good time to start "collecting" Ox images.

A fabulous wealth enhancer for this year is the **Asset Wealth Bull**. This Bull holds the symbolic and subliminal message "May the market bull for you"! With resplendent red saddle and surrounded by coins, ingots and symbols of prosperity, this bull energizes for wealth of the kind that can accumulate into expanded net worth, the kind that provides meaningful disposable income, providing a worry-free future.

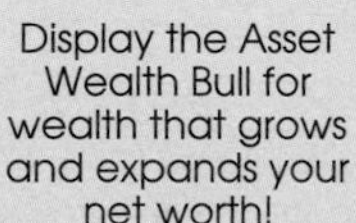

Display the Asset Wealth Bull for wealth that grows and expands your net worth!

To tap the hidden wealth of the year, display the **Ox finding Hidden Wealth**. This Ox is depicting calmly and unobtrusively grazing in a field full of coins, sniffing out hidden wealth and opportunities. In a year with little obvious wealth but a lot of hidden wealth, this Ox generates the luck that allows you to tap the full potential of the year.

Invite in the "Ox Finding Hidden Wealth" to tap the full potential of the year.

Another great activator for this year's wealth star is the **Tree Bringing 3 Kinds of Wealth**.

Trees always depict growth energy, and when they look like money trees, they really do bring the luck of wealth into the home! Our tree this year has been designed to represent the manifestation of 3 different kinds of wealth - Asset Wealth, Income Wealth and Growth Wealth. Having all three kinds of wealth brings you not just enough to lead a comfortable life now, it gives you security and peace of mind and allows you to plan for the future. This year's wealth tree also features 12 lucky charms to signify abundance in all forms entering your life - the Double Fish, the Apple, the Treasure Chest, the Golden Ingot, the Wealth Vase, the Abacus, the I-Ching Coin, Gold bars, the 4-leafed clover the Maneki Neko Lucky Cat and the Pot of Gold.

This year's wealth tree represents not just prosperity luck but also the luck of asset accumulation. This symbolises your wealth growing and your networth expanding.

Beware Betrayal & Loss Star *in the Northwest*

A dangerous aspect of this year's chart is the #7 Robbery Star in the NW. This brings loss and betrayal energies to the Patriarch, which not only means the patriarch of the family, but leaders, bosses, managers and anyone responsible for the welfare or livelihood of others. The presence of the #7 in the NW suggests that the Patriarch could get cheated, conned or betrayed. It brings the energy that suggests you should keep your friends close but your enemies closer.

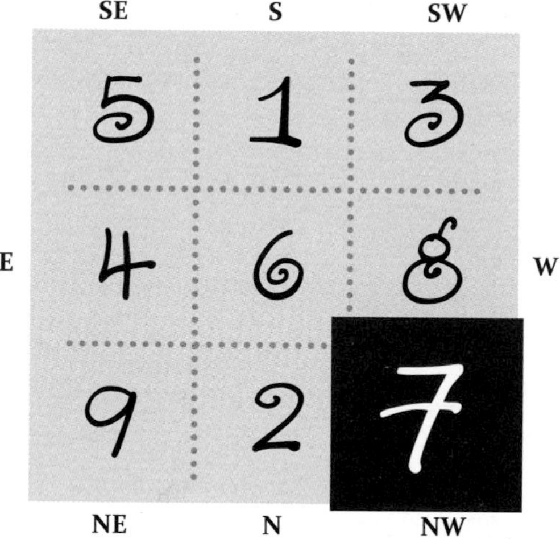

The NW, the sector of the Patriarch and Leader, gets afflicted by the #7 Loss and Betrayal Star in 2021.

In 2021, keep your friends close but your enemies closer!

Stay alert like a hawk, as treachery can strike at any moment. The energies of the year could corrupt even the most trustworthy of friends and the most loyal of employees. The #7 Robbery Star, like its namesake, describes a situation when you are cheated out of money; but it can also manifest as an actual robbery. We recommend all who stay out late, or who venture anywhere even remotely unsafe, to carry the **Nightspot Protection Amulet**. Because this star affects the NW, it harms the Father the most, but there can be knock-on adverse effects on the rest of the family, or the rest of a leader's charges.

CURE FOR #7 STAR: This year the best cure for the #7 star in the home is the **Anti-Burglary Plaque with Door Guardians.** These Door Gods with spear in the ready are depicted with the Anti-Burglary Amulets, with the Chinese proverb, "May your family be blessed with peace, safety and abundant joy, may your home be filled with everlasting happiness."

Display in the NW to ensure your home stays protected against unexpected and unwanted intruders, who may cause not just loss of property and possessions, but loss of peace of mind. These door guardians will help keep your family protected through the year.

BEWARE BETRAYAL:
This year, risk of betrayal is rife as the #7 star occupies the NW, the location of the leader. Betrayal means duplicity from those you trust, those you least suspect and therefore those you are most vulnerable to. While it feels nasty to get cheated by conmen and people you do not know, when betrayals come from those closest to you, the harm is emotional as well as physical. The loss is no longer merely monetary, it hits a nerve deep within that can be difficult to take and recover from. This year, because opportunity for this to happen gets increased, we suggest to remove temptation where you can, watch your back, and carry symbols to protect against this kind of bad luck. Carry the **Kuan Kung Anti-Betrayal Amulet**. This specially-designed talisman features the amulet that protects against being stabbed in the back, with the mantra that ensures the protection is effective.

PROTECT AGAINST BEING CHEATED:
For those engaging in high-risk deals carry the **Anti-Cheating Amulet** to ensure you do not get conned by unscrupulous people. An excellent amulet for business people and for anyone dealing with new acquaintances who maybe be untrustworthy.

PROTECTION AGAINST THE DARK ARTS:
Another form of harm can come from those who practice black magic. Especially in the East, such arts are more common than you think. Even if you do not subscribe or "believe" in this kind of power, it exists. Someone who projects negative thoughts against you, whether out of spite, jealousy or some other reason, does not even have to be skilled in these methods to send negative hexes and projectiles your way!

For example, if someone curses you on the street because they are angry at the way you drive, this can result in the same kind of misfortune effect as someone actively plotting or using black magic against you. The latter is of course more serious, but whenever one is weak in terms of spirit essence and element luck, they can succumb badly when someone forms negative thoughts and sends those thoughts their way.

The best protection against this kind of harm is the **28 Hums Protection Wheel**, which features the powerful **Heart Sutra** on the back. These sacred syllables together with this powerful sutra ensures that whatever projectiles are sent your way cannot reach you. A vital cure for anyone with enemies, who are engaged in high stakes deals, or anyone who may have offended someone intentionally or unintentionally.

28 Hums Protection Wheel

Suppress Illness Star
in the North

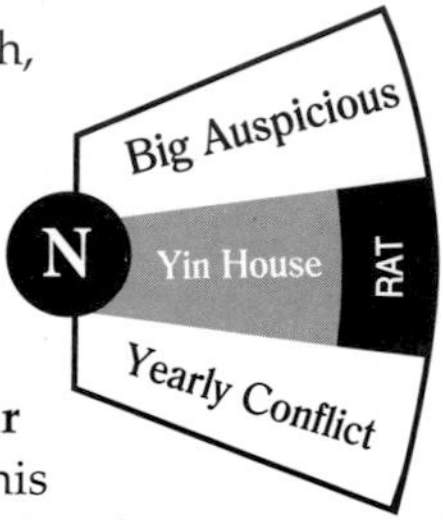

The #2 Illness Star flies to the North, and because North is of the Water element, it cannot do anything on its own to weaken the energies of the #2, an Earth star. The Illness Star is further strengthened as it is supported by the **Yin House Star** in North 2, the sector of the Rat. This boosts the potency of this star, making the North sector dangerous for those who are elderly, frail or prone to illness.

N
Big Auspicious
Yin House
RAT
Yearly Conflict

It is important for anyone whose bedroom is facing North, or whose home faces North to suppress the Illness Star with strong cures.

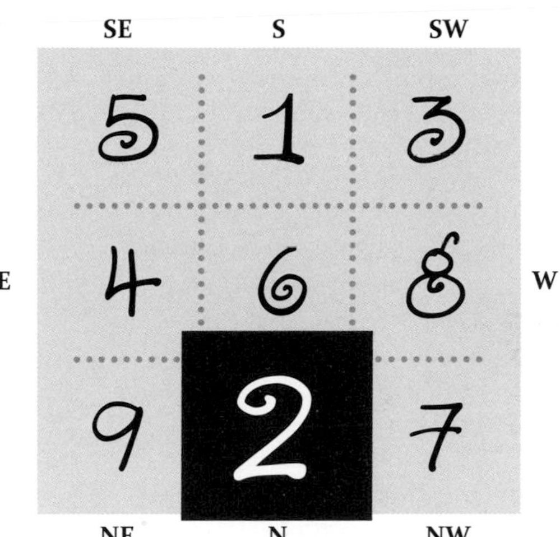

The North gets afflicted by the Illness Star this year.

CURE FOR THE ILLNESS STAR:

In 2021, a good cure for the Illness Star is the **Healing Deer Carrying Vase of Longevity with Linzhi**. The deer is renowned by the Chinese for their powerful curative properties and is often seen as the companion of the God of Longevity, Sau Seng Kong. With the world caught up in fears of epidemics and pandemics where there seems no escape with a proper cure a long time coming, the deer is an excellent shield against this kind of illness. Display in the North of the home this year. The Healing Deer is an excellent symbol of good health in the year 2021.

Another potent cure against the Illness Star #2 is the **Medicine Buddha and 7 Sugatas Gau**. Medicine Buddha always comes to the aid of those who are suffering when one calls for his help. His area of expertise is in the removal of poisons, disease and illness, and the **Medicine Buddha and 7 Sugatas Gau** features all 8 of his emanations, and his powerful mantras in whole. You can place in the North of the home to stay under his protection constantly. Excellent for anyone who is ill or feeling unwell.

You can also chant his mantra daily:
TADYATHA OM BHEKHANDZYE BHEKHANDZYE MAHA BHEKHANDZYE (BHEKHANDZYE) RADZA SAMUGATE SOHA

For those suffering from a chronic ailment, we suggest that you get yourself a dedicated **Medicine Buddha Mala** to chant with. The more you chant his mantra over the mala, the more powerful the mala will become. Keep the mala with you always, and whenever you have spare time, bring it out and chant. You can also wear the mala as an accessory around your wrist or neck.

AGAINST COVID-19:
To protect against the coronavirus specifically, the best cure is to invite in an image of the **Buddha Vairocana**, who brings blessings of good health but also provides strong protection against contagious diseases. Display his image as a figurine, and also carry his image in the form of a **Gold Talisman Card** which we have made available to help tide us through these challenging times.

AFFLICTIONS OF 2021
TAI SUI *in the NORTHEAST*

The TAI SUI or God of the Year always occupies the sector of the ruling animal sign of the year. This year, he occupies the palace of the Ox, Northeast 1. The Tai Sui is the celestial force that governs all that happens on Earth, and when one has his support and blessings, very little can go wrong, but when one offends him, his wrath knows no bounds.

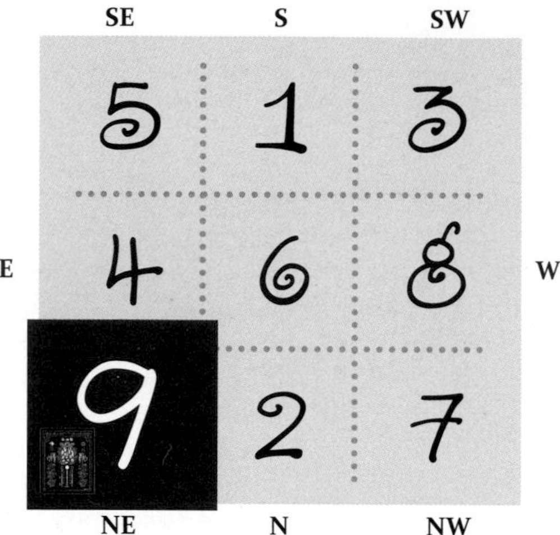

It is a matter of course and tradition for most Chinese who believe, to offer prayers to Tai Sui at the start of the year, humbly asking for his help and support for the coming year. In feng shui, the creature that is known to appease him is the celestial chimera the **Dragon Pi Xie**, so we always recommend to place this in the location of the Tai Sui.

The Dragon Pi Xie is said to appease the Tai Sui. Place in the NE in 2021.

PROTECTION: What is even more important is to place the **Tai Sui Plaque** with his image and invocation as a sign of respect. In 2021, place this in the NE1 sector. Animal signs especially affected by the Tai Sui this year are the Earth signs of **Sheep**, Dragon and Dog, while the Ox whose location he occupies should also be mindful of his presence there. For these 4 signs, we also recommend carrying the **Tai Sui Amulet** at all times throughout the year.

THREE KILLINGS in the EAST

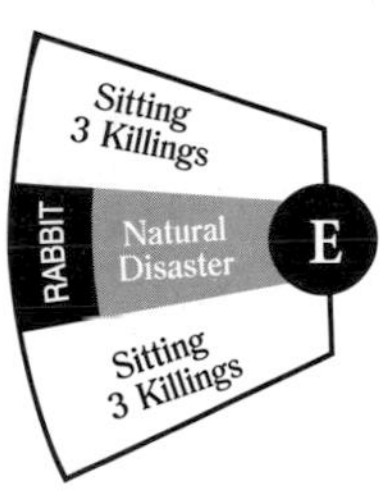

This affliction is said to bring three types of misfortune – loss of wealth, loss of reputation and loss of a loved one. All three are devastating, and when not one but three forms of bad luck hit you at once, the loss can be difficult and extremely distressing. This is another affliction that is important to take note of and to cure.

Firstly, NEVER have your back to the Three Killings affliction, so in 2021, DO NOT SIT FACING WEST,

There are also certain signs you need to stay alert to and wary of. One's Zodiac Adversary is the animal sign born six years apart from you, the sign directly opposite you in the Zodiac wheel – but in certain years, your "natural enemy" can become a useful ally, while in others, you would be best advised to stay well clear of each other. Having knowledge of how the year's energies influence your relationships will give you an edge when it comes to how you relate to others in any given year.

In this section, we analyse the relationship between the Sheep and the other signs in the Zodiac, looking in particular at the quality and nature of the relationships as determined by the influences of 2021.

1. Alliance of Allies

There are four affinity groupings that form natural allies in the horoscope. The three signs in each group have similar thought processes, aspirations and goals. Their attitudes are alike, and their support of each other is immediate and instinctive. If there is an alliance within a family unit amongst siblings, or between spouses and their child, the family is incredibly supportive, giving strength to each other. In good years, auspicious luck gets multiplied.

Astrological allies always get along. Any falling out is temporary. They trust each other and close ranks against external threats. Good astrological feng shui

ALLY GROUPINGS	ANIMALS	CHARACTERISTICS
Competitors	Rat, Dragon, Monkey	Competent, Tough, Resolute
Intellectuals	Ox, Snake, Rooster	Generous, Focused, Resilient
Enthusiasts	Dog, Tiger, Horse	Aggressive, Rebellious, Coy
Diplomats	Boar, Sheep, Rabbit	Creative, Kind, Emotional

comes from carrying the image of your allies, especially when they are going through good years.

When all three signs in a particular year has good fortune, the alliance is strengthened. But in years when one sign stands out with superior luck, the others in its grouping can "lean" on that sign to lift itself up. The Sheep belongs to the grouping of Diplomats in the Zodiac, comprising the Rabbit, Sheep and Boar.

This year, the strongest link in the Sheep's alliance of allies is the Rabbit, who has the most promising element luck in group For the Sheep, friends born in years of the Rabbit become a very good influence on you, and brings you good fortune luck.

In 2021, the Sheep can lean on the Rabbit to gain strength. It favours the Sheep to fraternize with friends born in the year of the Rabbit, who bring new opportunities to their ally the Sheep. The excellent element luck of your friend the Rabbit gives you a boost of confidence and a line to significant contacts and opportunities.

If you do not have close friends or alliances born in a Rabbit year, you can simulate this luck by displaying images or figurines of the Rabbit in your home. Hang beautiful and inspiring art of the Rabbit in your home, or display auspicious Rabbit depictions. The Rabbit when depicted with the moon attracts romance luck to singles and long-lasting happiness to those already married.

For the Sheep, displaying images of the Rabbit in your living space always brings romance and good fortune luck, and especially in 2021.

2. Zodiac Soulmates

Another natural ally for you is your Zodiac soulmate.In Chinese astrology, there are six pairs of signs that create six Zodiac Houses of yin and yang soulmates. Each pair creates powerful bonding on a cosmic level. Marriages or business unions between people belonging to the same Zodiac House are extremely auspicious. In a marriage, there is great love and devotion, and in a commercial partnership, it promises much wealth and success. Such a pairing is also good between professional colleagues or between siblings.

The strength of each pair is different, each having a defining strength with some making better commercial than marriage partners. How successful you are as a pair depends on how you bond. The table on the following page summarizes the key strength of each Zodiac house.

For the Sheep, your Zodiac Soulmate is the Horse. Together you form the *House of Passion & Sexuality*. Your relationship is characterized by passion and sexuality, so yours will be a highly-charged romantic affair, fuelled by your libidos. The Sheep gets carried away by the sexual overtures of the Horse, but being together also brings out your passion for some joint project or emotional cause that gets you both going.

In this partnership, the Horse embodies the male energy while the Sheep embodies the female energy. So you bring out the deeper sides of one another. Together you create *nien yen,* what Feng Shui Masters describe as excellent marriage and family luck, the kind that brings many descendants. A marriage between Sheep and Horse will have sexuality as the central focus that binds them, but the cosmic energy created will add much to your combined luck.

HOUSES OF PAIRED SOULMATES

ANIMALS	YIN/ YANG	ZODIAC HOUSE	TARGET UNLEASHED
Rat & Ox	YANG /YIN	***House of Creativity & Cleverness***	The Rat initiates The Ox completes
Tiger & Rabbit	YANG /YIN	***House of Growth & Development***	The Tiger uses strength The Rabbit uses negotiation
Dragon & Snake	YANG /YIN	***House of Magic & Spirituality***	The Dragon takes action The Snake creates magic
Horse & Sheep	YANG /YIN	***House of Passion & Sexuality***	The Horse embodies strength & courage The Sheep embodies seduction & allure
Monkey & Rooster	YANG /YIN	***House of Career & Commerce***	The Monkey creates good strategy The Rooster takes timely action
Dog & Boar	YANG /YIN	***House of Domesticity***	The Dog creates alliances The Boar benefits

3. Secret Friends

Another extremely powerful affinity arises when two secret friends come together. There are six pairs of secret friends in the Zodiac. Love, respect and goodwill flow freely between you. Once forged, your bond is extremely hard to break. Even when you yourselves want to break it, it will be hard for either party to walk away. This pair of signs will stick together through thick and thin.

For the Sheep, your secret friend is the Horse. This relationship is doubly special because the Horse is not just your secret friend, but your soulmate as well.

Sheep and Horse will be successful transforming every moment into something romantic and magical. You enjoy a happy family life constantly filled with new and happy surprises. The two of you will enjoy a special bond that others will envy. This will be a very happy pairing that

PAIRINGS OF SECRET FRIENDS	
Rat	Ox
Boar	Tiger
Dog	Rabbit
Dragon	Rooster
Snake	Monkey
Horse	Sheep

is especially helpful when one of you may be going through a hard time or when health issues cause one to lose energy or willpower to stick through a tough situation.

The secret friends pairing are like Zodiac best friends. Symbolically, the presence of your secret friend creates the chi of attracting good friends into your life.

4. Peach Blossom Links

Each alliance of allies has a special relationship with one of the four primary signs of Horse, Rat, Rooster and Rabbit in that these are the symbolic representations of love and romance for one alliance group of animal signs. These are referred to as Peach Blossom Animals, and the presence of their images in the homes of the matching alliance of allies brings peach blossom luck, which is associated with love and romance.

There is underlying passion between the Sheep and Rat. Because the Rat is your Peach Blossom link, displaying rats in the home brings love and marriage luck to the Sheep.

The Sheep belongs to the alliance of Rabbit, Sheep and Boar, which has the Rat as their Peach Blossom link.

The Sheep benefits from displaying images or paintings of the **Rat with Peach Blossom** in the North part of the house, or in the Sheep direction of SW.

5. Seasonal Trinities

Another grouping of signs creates the seasonal trinity combinations that bring the luck of *seasonal abundance*. To many experts, this is regarded one of the more powerful combinations. When it exists within a family made up of either parent or both parents with one or more children, it indicates that as a family unit, their collective luck can transform all that is negative into positive indications. When annual indications of the year are not favourable, the existence of a seasonal combination of signs in any living abode can transform bad luck into better luck, especially during the season indicated by the combination.

It is necessary for all three signs to live together or be in the same office working in close proximity for

ANIMAL SIGNS	SEASON	ELEMEMT	DIRECTION
Dragon, Rabbit, Tiger	*Spring*	Wood	East
Snake, Horse, Sheep	*Summer*	Fire	South
Monkey, Rooster, Dog	*Autumn*	Metal	West
Ox, Rat, Boar	*Winter*	Water	North

Seasonal Trinities

this powerful pattern to work. For greater impact, it is better if they are all using the direction associated with the relevant season. The Sheep belongs to the Summer Season, its direction is South, and its seasonal group comprises the Snake, Horse and Sheep.

6. Astrological Enemies

Your astrological enemy is the sign that directly confronts yours in the astrology wheel. For the Sheep, your astrological enemy is the Ox. Note that your enemy does not necessarily harm you; it only means someone of this sign can never be of any real help to you. There is a six year gap between natural enemies. A marriage between astroligical enemies is not usually recommended. Thus marriage between a Sheep and Ox is unlikely to bring lasting happiness unless other indications suggest otherwise. The Sheep is advised to refrain from getting involved with anyone born in the

PAIRINGS OF ASTROLOGICAL ENEMIES		
Rat	⟷	Horse
Boar	⟷	Snake
Dog	⟷	Dragon
Rabbit	⟷	Rooster
Tiger	⟷	Monkey
Ox	⟷	Sheep

year of the Ox, although on a year-by-year basis, this can sometimes be overcome by the annual energies. As a business partnership, this pairing is likely to lead to problems, and in the event of a split, the separation is often acrimonious and painful.

Sheep and Ox are better off not marrying or living together as partners. Even when there is love flowing back and forth during the initial stages, you are unlikely to be close over the long term. Note however that astrological opposites can co-exist quite harmoniously as friends or siblings.

If a Sheep is already married to an Ox, the solution to improve your prospects for lasting happiness is to introduce the secret friend of each other into your living space. This can be done through the symbolic use of figurines or art. As a pair, you should thus display the secret friend of the **Ox**, the **Rat**, and the secret friend of the **Sheep**, the **Horse**, in the home.

SHEEP with RAT

Peach Blossom link helps this relationship

Sheep and Rat are not naturally compatible. When together, each will need constant reassurance which neither has the patience to give. There is a tendency for both to be selfish when it comes to the other. As a couple, they tend to show each other up, which plays on insecurities and makes neither look good. Their differing attitudes cause this to be a problematic match.

The energies of 2021 make this pairing even more difficult. Sheep is under the influence of the argumentative star, and Rat who is lacking in energy will not have the patience to argue.

Should they meet and be physically attracted to one another, as long as they keep things casual, the relationship could prove exciting for a while. Sheep is the seductress of the Zodiac, and when it turns on the charm, it is difficult for anyone to resist, least of all the earnest Rat. But when things begin to get serious, their incompatibilities become too pronounced. It is difficult for Sheep and Rat to discuss anything serious with one another, as they just don't respect each other enough. Any attempt at conversation about anything of real consequence quickly falls apart, so once any physical attraction between them wears off, there is little left to form the basis of a lasting relationship.

The one consolation is that the Rat is the Peach Blossom link of the Sheep. Romance can thus blossom between them. But it will be one-sided, with Sheep getting the better end of the deal. Leave these two long enough and Rat would most likely want out.

Sheep and Rat do better in a work situation. As long as emotions are not involved, their differing approaches could find an advantageous fit. But when they allow themselves to get too close, there could well be arguments galore with neither side backing down. And if they find themselves in any kind of competition with one another, things could get quite ugly.

This relationship can work if one or the other are clearly in charge. If Sheep and Rat are parent and child, boss and employee, teacher and student, there is no problem. Rat can be extremely nurturing of Sheep and vice versa. But when both come to the relationship as equals, there is too little compatibility for things to work out. Sheep is too gentle and relaxed for the Rat, and Rat is too excitable for the Sheep.

SHEEP with OX

Astrological adversaries

Sheep and Ox are an unlikely pair under regular circumstances, but 2021 makes this coupling even more disastrous. They are incompatible on almost every level. Being natural adversaries of the Zodiac, a match between them is never recommended unless other variables are present that point to compatibility. Their personalities just don't click, and the energies of the year make this mismatch even more pronounced.

Sheep and Ox will rarely see eye-to-eye, and in 2021, the quarrelsome star afflicting the Sheep makes matters worse. If together, this pair is likely to face conflict after conflict, until one or the other decides that enough is enough.

These two never make a good match, and this year will only serve to accentuate this fact. Their Earth energies, rather than coming together in productive fashion, will result in major clashes over and over. They are competitive with one another and find it difficult to genuinely applaud each other's successes. Both need to be going through equally good times to appreciate one another, but the coming year is luckier for the Ox than the Sheep. A Sheep and Ox couple could thus see Sheep growing resentful if its Ox partner continues to enjoy individual success; in this case, Sheep may cause drama and discord, even if unintentially. There will be little harmony in a Sheep-Ox household. If already married, they will need to bring in an **image of the Rat** and **Horse**, and place in the SW and NE sectors respectively. This will help ease tensions between them.

At work, Sheep and Ox are not the best of allies unless they stay at arm's length with one another. Ox views Sheep as manipulative, while Sheep despises Ox's dictatorial ways. It is difficult for each to recognise the other's positive traits, so the relationship is doomed from the first instant. Both will need to work very hard to make things work.

FENG SHUI CURE: If Sheep and Ox find themselves in a situation where they have no choice but to work with one another, they will need the **Earth Cross**. Display the **Mirror Building Solid Foundations** somewhere within easy view. This cross featuring all four Earth signs of Ox, Sheep, Dragon and Dog will transform animosity into support, and hostility into goodwill, helping build a strong foundation for Ox and Sheep to work from.

SHEEP with TIGER  

Marriage of convenience

Tiger and Sheep do not make an expected couple. There is little natural attraction between these two because their personalities, life views and aspirations are so different. Tiger's extroverted nature comes across brash and unrefined to the genteel Sheep, and Sheep's conventional outlook appears dull and unexciting to the Tiger. But these two may well come together in marriage if it is one of convenience.

While their outward appearances may differ, and similarly their life goals, they are both intensely shrewd and astute types who are willing to forgo passion and pleasure if they believe their ultimate aims are worth it. They may marry each other for money, or for rank, for instance.

But 2021 makes even this kind of attraction difficult. Sheep is quarrelsome and quick-tempered with the influence of the *Argument Star*. Tiger meanwhile is on a roll filled with momentum and energy, and loses interest quickly, and most certainly won't easily put up with Sheep's temper tantrums.

Tiger will want to dominate the relationship, and while Sheep is happy for Tiger to play frontman, it will want to pull the strings from the background. And Tiger will not like this. This relationship will only work if Sheep can give something of real value to the Tiger, whether in terms of family connections, superior strategy or funding. It will not be a marriage where love is a priority. And yes, one can build a stable and even successful family life together on this basis, but sooner or later, one or the other will stray.

Infidelity can quickly come to characterise this union, and if found out, the other will not quickly forgive. With the energies of 2021's *External Star of Romance*, this pair is at highest risk of becoming a victim of third party disturbances. When arguments are blowing up, temptation outside the marriage becomes difficult to resist.

This pair works better on a platonic level, where emotions do not come into play. But even then, there is a distinct lack of excitement. These two signs are unlikely to form any kind of meaningful union with one another.

FENG SHUI CURE: If already married and you want to ensure your marriage stay protected against infidelity and betrayal, you should have the **Marriage Happiness Ducks** in the SW of the home, and carry the **Enhancing Relationship Amulet**.

SHEEP with RABBIT

Much love between two soulmates

Sheep and Rabbit are two kindred spirits able to really wax lyrical about all the finer things in life and enjoy them together. This is a couple who are sure to work out well, as they find beauty and value in exactly the same things. It is like they are of one mind when they indulge themselves. They are like a match made in heaven making beautiful music together.

They get their highs discovering new experiences together and are able to create their own world where love flows freely between them. They get bored at the same kinds of things and are stimulated by similar experiences. So here we see an emotional and artistic affinity flowering into deep and abiding love. This couple are certain to become soul mates capable of bringing great happiness to each other.

2021 sees Rabbit in the mood for romance, while Sheep has the quarrelsome star affliction, but in each other's arms, the cares of the world melt away and they constantly lift each other's spirits.

Rabbit may have to work a bit harder in light of Sheep's pricklier disposition in 2021, but with these two, arguments usually get put out before they grow into anything big. If Sheep is mad with the world, rather than fight with a Rabbit partner, Rabbit is more likely to jump to Sheep's defence and they fight the sins of the world together. They are there for each other through thick and thin, and forgive each other anything.

These two are genuine allies, looking out for each other and creating easy rapport and comradeship.

Whether the relationship is romantic or platonic, there is always great warmth and affection. As work colleagues or business partners, they get along like a house on fire, so it rarely feels like work. But they can be mighty productive together, as both are responsible types who do not let distractions affect productivity.

As workmates, there is risk this year of Sheep and Rabbit hooking up romantically but illicitly. If each are separately happily married to other people, a passionate affair may lead to emotional complications, not to mention professional ones, so it is a good idea to be aware of such risks. They will enjoy it for sure, but an illicit tryst may not be worth endangering everything for. And don't think it will be a casual one-time fling, because between these two, once something begins, it will not just end. Their connection runs too deep for that.

SHEEP with DRAGON

Uncomfortable relationship where both are quarrelsome

These are two Earth signs that can work in a conducive year, but 2021 is not such a year. These two make for a vibrant relationship when one clearly dominates. They are also better when each are pursuing their own thing. When they lead separate lives as well as the one they share with one another, their union can blossom into a long-lasting partnership.

In truth, they do not have all that much in common. It is easy to list their differences, as these tend to be many and wide-ranging. Their styles differ, as do their aspirations and values. They look at life and the world through different lenses. And so, often, when they attempt to walk the same road, it is like walking a road to nowhere. And sooner or later, they realise this and could well be tempted to part ways.

They are not helped in 2021 as Sheep is troubled by the quarrelsome star, making it more irritable than usual. Dragon does nothing to soothe its tempers, so things get noisy and heated in a Sheep and Dragon pairing this year.

When both go through good years, these two can make for a beautiful union, as Sheep is in awe of Dragon's magnetism and charisma, while Dragon gets roped in by Sheep's seductive ways. There will also be no tussle for control, as Sheep happily yields to Dragon's natural dominance.

In years like this one, both may tend to act out of character as they are hardly helped by the energies afflicting them. The Dragon is more fiery than usual, and so is the Sheep. Gone then is the dreamy elegance that they can share in the early stages of a courtship.

If Sheep and Dragon meet this year, it is unlikely that any real attraction will take root. They simply cannot recognise all that is positive in each other.

Things are better between them in a work relationship, especially when they do not get too close or too comfortable with one another. They are different enough to bring their varied skills and talents to the mix, and the result could result in much success and productivity. But because of the quarrelsome energies in the air, it is better if one is clearly the boss. When you put a Sheep and Dragon together on equal footing, the year may see them butt heads more frequently than working in tandem.

SHEEP with SNAKE

Snake pacifies the Sheep this year

These two may not make the most obvious pair on the surface, but they have more in common than at first glance. While Sheep appears more sentimental and Snake more detached, these are two deeply emotional and spiritual signs that can find the most brilliant of connections if circumstances allow.

When Sheep and Snake are in the same line of work, interested in the same hobbies, or thrown together by a turn of fate, they can build an extremely lasting and meaningful bond with one another.

Snake is of the Fire element and Sheep of the Earth element, so it will be Snake that tends to sustain the relationship. In 2021, both have afflictive stars - Sheep has the quarrelsome star and Snake has the *Five Yellow*, but both have a *Big Auspicious* star each, bringing real promise to their year together.

A Snake battling a personal complication will appreciate Sheep's kind and sympathetic ear, while a Sheep going through something similar will value Snake's practical solutions to its problems. While their approaches to life's setbacks may be different, when they combine, the outcomes are really very good. A

Snake and Sheep pair work almost better when there are problems to face than when everything is smooth sailing.

In 2021, both Sheep and Snake meet with issues they would rather not have to deal with, but with each other as partner or teammate, they imbue each other with courage, hope and strength. Sheep may find itself more irritable this year, but a Snake mate always manages to calm it down. These two may not have obvious affinities, but the ones they do have are far more important than things like superficial tastes, goals or aspirations.

The Snake this year is surrounded by an aura of attraction that pulls in the Sheep, and a Snake and Sheep pair that develops romantic feelings for each other can look forward to a passionate year indeed! When together, they view the world through rose-tinted glasses and are able to forget their problems while bathed in their infatuation with each other.

Ironically, that may be just what both need - to forget their woes temporarily. When they face their problems with a happy disposition, they find much better solutions, and problems then quickly solve themselves. A beneficial pairing!

SHEEP with HORSE

Intermittent hostility but emerging stronger

Although Sheep and Horse share an astrologically closely linked and deep relationship with one another, in 2021 they could nevertheless experience verbal clashes. While they have strong ties, the energies this year bring very quarrelsome energies the way of the Sheep, and these two share an intensely passionate rapport where everything gets enhanced.

Their feelings and emotions, when it has to do with each other, get magnified out of proportion, and whatever they feel, either positive or negative, they express tenfold to each other.

In 2021, it would appear that together or individually they have a lot of latent hostility energy to deal with. They need an extraordinary store of patience and plenty of goodwill to ride through a stormy year ahead. And even with strong feng shui cures in place, it is likely there will be intermittent hostility causing unhappiness and a great deal of aggravation.

FENG SHUI CURE: The way to smooth the year for this pair is to use the power of **Fire energy** and to **wear red** as much as possible.

Soulmates ★★★★★

Sheep and Horse have the ability to make each other extremely happy. They think in the same way and are also physically very compatible. They are able to please each other and to establish good foundations for long-term happiness. Their attraction is rooted in their attitudes which complement each other.

The Zodiac is bullish about a Sheep and Horse pairing as this couple are not just secret friends but also soulmates as they share the same Zodiac house, that of sexuality and passion, with Horse exuding the male yang energy and Sheep creating the female yin energy. This translates to suggest complete compatibility. They have a special relationship that is strong and enduring and that can last the long haul. Horse is upfront and courageous and Sheep is constant and stable. Horse likes to lead and take charge, and this is just fine with the gentle, easy-going Sheep. Between them is a big store of goodwill.

2021 may mess up their passionate and idyllic existence a little, as tempers will tend to flare, but Sheep and Horse always make up quickly after a fight, and sometimes this makes them even stronger. There is no doubt that Sheep and Horse can build a very happy and successful marriage or partnership together, even if this year may not be their best one.

SHEEP with MONKEY

A matching of minds but quarrelsome

While Sheep and Monkey fall at two different ends of the emotional divide, one being extremely emotional and the other very analytical, they can easily become the best of pals. Their approach to life is different and so are their personalities, but there is real attraction between them with the old adage of opposites attracting holding true. Sheep admires Monkey's quick, agile brain, while Monkey finds Sheep's diplomatic ways admirable and endearing.

In 2021, Monkey benefits from the demeanour of the Sheep, who is excellent at making friends and influencing people. Sheep meanwhile enjoys the refuge provided by Monkey's ingenuity. On balance, this is potentially a very beneficial match.

There is danger however of Sheep getting hurt by Monkey's tendency towards insensitivity, and in 2021, this could well happen as both are afflicted by the year's hostility star. There is every likelihood that Monkey will take Sheep for granted, and when this happens, there could develop misunderstandings that get so severe and serious they could end up causing real harm to each other.

Those already married to each other must understand that there is great imbalance of energy between them in 2021. Monkey has extremely strong element luck, with enough chi energy to hold the union or partnership together. Sheep lags behind in terms of element energy, and Monkey could often find itself getting frustrated at Sheep's more leisurely and languid pace.

Both are more than a match for each other and that is why this match works so well, but 2021 puts Monkey on higher footing, which works only if Sheep is happy to submit. This will not always be the case, and that is when the quarrels could erupt.

Both are extremely clever individuals, so are unlikely to cross over into hazardous territory with each other, but with the Quarrelsome Star hovering, they could well come close. This year then, there may well be distractions and hiccups along the way, but no lasting damage will take place if both make an effort to resolve differences before they become irreconciliable.

FENG SHUI CURE: It is a good idea for Monkey and Sheep who are together to each carry **Anti-Conflict Amulets** to suppress the destructive effects of the hostility star, which affects you both this year.

SHEEP with ROOSTER

Making waves together in 2021

While Sheep and Rooster may be very different personalities, and will occasionally have their clashes, when a Sheep and Rooster pairing works, it can be wonderful indeed! They work better in a non-romantic setting, although in love and marriage, if they can find a happy balance, there is no reason why they cannot build a good life and future together.

In 2021, Sheep and Rooster's luck stars combine to form the natural leader Ho Tu, which indicates that should they come together in a work or business situation this year, or as political couple or team, they can attain great success.

As a pair, they can set new trends, change opinions and make a real difference to the world. These are both highly opinionated individuals, and because both often insist they are right, when their opinions diverge, quarrels may emerge. If neither side gives way is when the problems will start. So in the long run, a marriage between a Sheep and Rooster could be filled with irritability and temper tantrums. But when they are working together on a joint goal, such outbursts could provide the creative basis for some brilliant work to get done. If they do come together in a close relationship, a deep connection can be formed. Their personalities may not align like the perfect jigsaw, but there is genuine respect from both sides, indicating a pairing that can last.

2021 will be a great year for these two signs should they join forces. Usually it is the Rooster who is bossy with a take-charge attitude that could rile the Sheep, but this year the tables may turn, when Sheep is the one whose mood swings threaten to upset the apple cart. But if any sign this year can appease the Sheep, it will be the empathetic Rooster.

In this union, Rooster will tend to take the lead, and Sheep will be more than happy to follow. Of the two, Rooster is the more organised and disciplined, while Sheep provides the inspiration. One may end up becoming the other's muse.

Because Rooster's element luck is much stronger than Sheep's in 2021, it will be Rooster driving the team effort, propping up the Sheep and keeping things moving forward. But with a Rooster partner, Sheep's *Big Auspicious* indication has every chance of blossoming nicely into fruition.

SHEEP with DOG

A happy pairing in 2021

Sheep and Dog enjoy a moderate affinity with one another. While not entirely compatible, with differing personalities and life goals, these two signs can make a relationship between them work because they can agree to disagree. Neither side is particularly insistent on taking charge, so they will share the honours. While there may not be any grand passion here, they can make a very cordial and accomodating pair.

In 2021, these two Earth signs are helped by their luck stars, which combine to bring them much shared good fortune.

In work and business, Sheep and Dog make great strides together in the coming year. They are more productive and find each other a good sounding board whenever they need to formulate strategy and new ideas. Sheep's creativity gets a great boost with the loyal Dog's constant applause.

The nice thing about this relationship is the lack of jealousy or malice. They never feel like that towards each other. Even when pitted against each other for any reason, they can wear two hats - that of competitors as well as supporters. Neither is a sore loser, nor does one insist on taking the credit or hogging the limelight.

In a love relationship, things are easier if the stakes in any difference of opinion are not too high. It also helps if the Sheep allows the Dog to make the difficult decisions, and is able to fall in with plans submissively.

In socialising with outside parties however, both Sheep and Dog are excellent in keeping friends and making others feel comfortable, so as a couple, they will be popular with an extensive network of contacts and allies. So life together is usually pleasant.

This pair should enjoy a relatively harmonious year with no major disruptions. There is good affinity in their energies and for once, they are communicating on the same wavelength as there is much common ground. Indeed, there is more that link them than pull them apart.

While this may not be a usual pairing, things are helped very much in 2021 by the annual energies. If Sheep and Dog fall in love this year, romance will play a big part. You don't get any sign as romantic as the dreamy Sheep. The nice thing in this union is that Dog will appreciate all of Sheep's thoughtfulness and advances. There is plenty of mutual attraction here.

SHEEP with BOAR 

Enjoying completion luck together

Sheep and Boar always get along. They are a happy and compatible couple with plenty of natural affinity. Whether they have known each other for years or have only just met, there is an easy camraderie between them. Conversation flows freely and they enjoy the same things. This pair has great and obvious love for each other and their instinctive congeniality to each other make them restful and comfortable in one another's presence.

In 2021, their relationship gets further enhanced as their luck stars combine to form the lucky sum-of-ten. What they start together, they complete with great success.

Their natural affinity to each other is infectious, enabling them to overcome almost anything they have to face. As a couple, they win many supporters and friends, and they will never be short of people wanting to help them. They make a dynamo team in work matters, and they build a very happy family life as a married couple. Both have similar goals, and their attitudes sync up without one ever having to convince the other over anything.

This year Sheep is afflicted by the Quarrelsome Star, but in the company of the Boar, Sheep's tempers are soothed. Both are amiable personalities, although the Sheep can have a sting, which the Boar successfully neutralises every time.

Sheep and Boar make up two thirds of the group of allies described as the *Diplomats* of the Zodiac. They share a gentle disposition, and their lifestyle mirrors their desire for a quiet and elegant existence. When these two get together, you can be assured they know how to enjoy life. In fact, they will hone each other's expensive tastes in food, wine, holidays and experiences.

But Sheep and Boar are disciplined individuals who will put in the work without a fuss if they need to. Not for these two making money for money's sake. No, for them, they will likely spend a large proportion of what they earn.

This year promises love, passion and desires fulfilled for Sheep and Boar couples who are married. Their luck holds strong and affect both positively. Sheep has stronger element luck than Boar, so Sheep will be the one driving this relationship in 2021. But whichever of the two is in charge does not matter, because the other will happily give its full support.

will let up. Tackle work in manageable bites. Spend time organizing yourself and ask for help you need it. If you put effort into planning, you will find a way to get everything done more effectively and in less time. Resist the temptation to stay long hours at the office. Working late too many consecutive nights could end up being counterproductive, slowing you down rather than speeding you up. And when you're overly tired, you could make costly careless mistakes.

Take a break from your career aspirations, even if a short one. Getting the rest and respite you need now will make you more effective when you tune back in.

Business - *Take a break*

You have a lot on your mind making it difficult to concentrate. Don't worry over minor issues. You're not feeling in the pink of health, so even small tasks can seem major. Make time for a break or vacation; even a little time off can make all the difference! Put more trust in others, especially your own people. You have to let go of the reins once in a while, and this year unfortunately more often than you are used to. If you spend more time training others rather than fixing things yourself every time something goes wrong, you'll build up a more effective organization. If your health is telling you to slow down, listen. Taking a pause won't hamper you; it will speed you up in the larger scheme of things.

Love & Relationships - *Fulfilling!*

Romance, unlike your work life, is flourishing, and single Sheep get a good shot at love. It's all systems go as far as love is concerned! You may meet someone who matches all your criteria. Even if you fail to meet the right person, you will definitely have fun doing it! Married Sheep reconnect with their spouses in a special way, making life more fulfilling. Your partner can influence you in unexpected but delightful ways and you can go as deep as you wish with their suggestions.

Family & Friendships - *Catching up*

A good time to reconnect with family whether immediate or distant relatives. Even if single and living out of town, make an effort to return to the family home to catch up with your folks. They will be so pleased to see you and if one is ailing, your presence will act as a tonic no doctor can give!

School & Education - *Don't get cocky*

You are motivated for all the right reasons. You have the support of your peers and teachers and have good study and exam luck. So seems like you are sorted. Refrain from being cocky if there are disagreements with classmates while working on projects. You may be right on all counts, but a little courtesy goes a long way.

CURE FOR THE MONTH: Carry **Medicine Buddha's Amulet** or **Medicine Buddha's Mantra Wand** to remove health obstacles this month.

2nd Month
March 6th - April 4th 2021

LUCK IMPROVES. SOME VERY POSITIVE DEVELOPMENTS.

As you move further into the Ox year, it certainly becomes more friendly for you. The Sheep enjoys new beginnings this month, making this a time when you can start new projects with high chance of success. Whatever you set in motion now will deliver delightful rewards either now or soon. This is an auspicious period as the stars favour all sorts of new things, whether a new business, new range of products or new offices. This also extends to planting new trees and buying new items at great prices! A good time to refresh your wardrobe, give your home a spring clean, and throw out things you no longer have a use for.

Work & Career - *Many rewards*

Work brings many rewards in the form of extra money, higher status or even a new title which can be a job title or one bestowed by the authorities! An auspicious time in store as you are like a bud about to burst into full bloom with all petals fully extended! New projects land in your lap and they represent opportunities to show how well you can handle responsibilities. Your power of communications are world class and you are in demand for front line work where you have to meet or liase with people whose first contact with your company will be you. If first impressions count, then surely you are 'it'!

You are a natural choice when a leader is needed this month, as people respect you, and you can easily marshall everyone over to your side.

Business - *Growth energy*

A month that encourages new things and promotes organic growth, so you must exploit it by expanding your range of products and services, hire more staff, expand and diversify. Joint ventures and partnerships are favoured. Touch base with your important contacts. You wield more power than you presume, so follow up on leads and persuade influential people to invest in your schemes. Even if minor obstacles crop up, they are easily removed, so keep trucking and you could well hit the bigtime. Your luck holds so you can afford to take some risks in the stock market. If you invest in second liners and make money, sell and cash out. Don't become greedy as this is easy money. Donate to charity if you win big to ensure you can maintain your gains.

Love & Relationships - *Feeling good*

A new group of friends enter your life and some are very attractive. You are confused as to who is the right one, but this is one of life's wonderful puzzles, so you should enjoy yourself while solving this conundrum! Remember, love can be found in the strangest of places and under the most unexpected of conditions! You see stars this month and almost everyone takes an instant liking to you too. The Sheep is the most seductive sign in the Chinese Horoscope, and this month those powers come to the fore. But despite the easy temptations of the flesh, you are not too hot on ships sailing through the night, preferring long term prospects. Choose carefully before committing though.

Education - *On a roll*

You are on a roll now when your results are good and your hard work is finally being recognized! You demonstrate great leadership and others know a leader when they see one. If you stand for election for any position, you win easily. Your sharp mental state now demands you push the envelope and test your limits. Balance schoolwork with other activities and you're laying all the right groundwork for the future.

ENHANCER FOR THE MONTH:
You benefit greatly from the **Victory Banner Success Amulet**. Those chasing scholarships should keep the **Manjushri "Dhih" Scholastic Amulet** close.

3rd Month
April 5th - May 5th 2021

PACE PICKS UP. MAKING SOLID PLANS FOR THE FUTURE.

Last month was good, but this month matches it for your enthusiasm, luck, energy and drive. In fact, you're feeling even more pumped and motivated because you've sorted out your commitments, leaving you more time to make new plans for the future. You are bursting with passionate vibes so you can now build your team, get people on your side, source funding for your projects. Invest in confidence, even take some risks. Just watch you do not brush people up the wrong way, as the *Quarrelsome Star* gets enhanced by the visiting *Magnification Star*. If there is something on your mind, better to have an outlet. Don't let uneasy feelings fester. If something doesn't feel right, talk about it.

Work & Career - *Keeping busy*

You are happy provided you have plenty to sink your teeth into, and this month, there is plenty to do. The busier you are, the more contented you feel, a sure-fire sign of a workaholic except it's not permanent for better or worse! Someone in your workplace may try sabotage you, but you are in the mood to wage war and of course you win hands down! You give as good as you get but try to maintain your integrity at all times. Round up support from colleagues as you will need them when the time comes. You not only succeed in most of your projects but are also perceived to be a winner. People hang on to your every word, so you have strong support. Just don't let such transient flattery go to your head. And if you've spotted an enemy, stay wary in the future, even if you've won this round.

You enjoy the company of others and likewise for them. Use this time to network. Friendships developed now will last long and also help you professionally.

Business - *Rethinking plans*

Rethinking existing business plans is advisable; perhaps new strategies to beat the competition that may be causing you some sweat. A few offbeat ideas may be what you need, since you have gone through the tried and tested. Avoid public confrontations with angry clients or dissatisfied partners - any such bickering will bounce back on you later. Revenues may dip, but this is temporary, so don't blame yourself too much. A good month for networking and making contacts. Lay the groundwork for future expansion but delay official signings till next month.

Love & Relationships - *Sizzling*

A scorching time for lovers and those conducting an affair! Good time to take a break and go on holiday! Perhaps a weekend escapade to some romantic beach where you can strip to swim gear or some cooler climes where you can huddle and cuddle. Go all out to pursue the person of your dreams if you are convinced they are the right one. Those single and looking could meet attractive potential suitors of all manner. And the best thing, you don't have to try very hard at all because they all seem to flock to you! You can seduce nearly anyone by turning on the charm and the person will find you irresistible; you have the magic now! Enjoy it!

Education - *Accolades*

The young Sheep is shining bright. Your earlier efforts are now getting recognised. Some may win awards or scholarships or other accolades. A month of recognition. If you're working on your CV, there are plenty of opportunities to add to your growing list of achievements. If you haven't built up an impressive enough resumé, now is the time to change that.

ENHANCER FOR THE MONTH: Carry the **Windhorse Success Amulet** to boost success potential this month. Best to also have the **Apple Peace Amulet** to keep the magnified #3 star under control.

Peace

Don't put too much energy into trying to overcome the competition. Instead, focus on improving your own product and service, and results will come. You have great ideas but need to back these up with a solid strategy. Aim high when your luck levels are high. As they are now.

Love & Relationships - *Make your move*

You exude a very positive air which makes you popular with everyone you meet. Existing friendships also benefit from your wonderful attitude. When it comes to love, don't let opportunities pass you by. It's too easy to be passively receiving compliments and waiting for others to make a move, but if there's someone you have your eye on, go for it! You only need to give an indication and they will respond. But wait too long and someone else could get there first, and then you've missed your chance.

Home & Family - *Compromising*

There may be differences in opinions between you and the older generations, but nothing you can't solve without some deft compromising.

Education - *Love your work*

If studying topics of interest, your talent and potential knows no bounds. The secret is to make yourself love whatever it is you are studying. Yes, it's totally possible to make yourself love your syllabus, as opposed to looking for something to study that you love. It is all in the mindset.

5th Month
June 6th - July 6th 2021

COMPLETION LUCK. BUT BEWARE BETRAYALS.

The sum-of-ten gets formed by the visiting Loss Star and the resident Quarrelsome Star, so even though individual stars point to trouble, things end well. Life may not all be smooth sailing, but if you keep the faith and leave it to the divine hands of fate, everything works out. The Sheep however is an emotional sign, so it won't be easy to merely be a passenger to events unfolding. You'll want to seize back control and right the wrongs that appear to be taking place before your eyes. One of these will come in the form of betrayal. Even though your wrongdoer may not cause you actual harm, the incident is likely to taint your relationship; unless you can bring yourself to believe the disloyalty was an inevitable result of the feng shui flying stars.

Work & Career - *Beware jealousies*

Work is relatively smooth as you are very simpatico with everyone in the office and still enjoy goodwill lingering from previous months. Everyone values your opinion, but beware of petty jealousies. This time you are more vulnerable to gossip and backstabbing. Deal with such politicking by displaying a **Rooster with Crown** on your desk. You are swamped with commitments but if you plan carefully and stick to your pre-planned timetable, you can achieve a lot.

Business - *Defining moments*

You enjoy some defining moments which can affect your bottomline for ages to come. This is considered an auspicious period so do put enough attention on work-related activities. Some big deals in the pipeline that allow you to breathe easy for a while. But there's a chance of being used by unscrupulous agents or even being cheated outright, so this is the time to look sharp. Don't be sloppy when signing deals and documents. In your zest, you may overlook the fine print. Legal problems can surface later so avoid nasty surprises by counter checking with lawyers. Check the background of those you are going into business with, and don't simply jump onboard lest the ship turns out to contain leaks.

Double-check everything you do. Don't take chances. Good fortune luck, but tainted by the risk of being cheated by someone you know and trust.

Love & Relationships - *Stagnant*

Your love life is rather stagnant. Even if attached, you feel you might as well be single at the rate your spouse or lover showers you with attention! You also pick little fights for no valid reason. Even if the other party is to blame, you surely will not feel any happier for that. If you want to continue, you have to be the one making all the moves and taking the initiative. This might become too much even for someone whose patience is legendary. It might even get to the stage where you feel it simply cannot work and perhaps it is time to say sayonara. Maybe the other side will be grateful too!

Friendships - *Misunderstandings*

Friendships suffer from misunderstandings, so you are beginning to see the merits of being a hermit. You're not totally yourself, so maybe take a break from too much socialising. The detox could you do you good!

Education - *Conflict energies*

Conflicts arise with at least one student. Be less aggressive or you will antagonize more! You may have to endure some gossip, though you can be both victim and the one doing the gossiping. Either way won't be pleasant. If you want to keep your friends, don't push them into a corner. Sometimes you think you are doing it in their interest, but unless they share your view, they will be resentful. Study luck is average as you have too many things on your mind.

CURE FOR THE MONTH: Carry the **Anti-Cheating Amulet with Kuan Kung** to stay protected against the #7 Star and to safeguard against getting cheated by unscrupulous people in the course of doing business.

6th Month
July 7th - Aug 7th 2021

HEAVEN LUCK HELPING YOU. A MENTOR MAKES AN APPEARANCE.

Heaven luck descends on you, taking away some of the worries conjured up last month. Things fall back into place with an invisible hand guiding you. Your instincts kick back into action, making you more decisive once more. Even if you're not fully confident inside, you have enough conviction now to follow your heart. You enjoy heavenly chi, which keeps opening new doors for you even when old ones close. Don't dwell on the past; keep moving forward. If you spend your time regretting bad decisions of the past, you won't have time to focus on making good ones for the future. The Sheep also enjoys mentor luck; someone in a high position takes you under their wing to help you. If you accept that help with open arms, you can rise through the ranks very quickly.

Work & Career - *Taking credit*

Since you perform so well, you deserve all the accolades piling up. Everyone thinks all the good things are due to you. Don't shy away from taking the credit but be prepared to share it. There is no need however to be too self-deprecating. This is your moment to shine, so seize it! You look forward to work each day, as you are appreciated, and your career path seems clear and going the way you intended. You enjoy strong support from your bosses, and you can get very close to them if you wish, so make the most of the situation. You are feeling exceptionally creative which takes you far at this time. Certain things you say or do contain great gems of brilliance. Enhance goodwill by working on your relationships among colleagues and you will be seen as an indispensable team player.

Business - *Invaluable network*
Your network of friends, contacts and business associates prove handy! Your luck is good but you still have to work for wealth. Examine all opportunities that come your way. There are some winners among them, so don't dismiss any. You can expand, invest and spend as much as you think is necessary, as the more you reach out, the more you are rewarded. If you need some connections to get things done, you are able to do so as you now have some powerful strings to pull. This is also the time to call for favours as it's payback time!

Someone unexpected may emerge and play an influential role. He or she will be a guiding light and a blessing to your prospects.

Love & Relationships - *Joyous*

A great month as everywhere you look, someone dishy seems to be waving at you! You can be as frivolous, fun and fickle as you like, as your admirers are prepared to tolerate you to the max. Let the real you come out a bit and you can party like there is no tomorrow! Let your hair down as you can get away with most things. If you are married or in a relationship, someone has to take the lead. If you assume that role, it will be even more exciting, since you are the one with the golden touch. This is a great time to get engaged or married as joyous occasions will create even more powerful, positive chi that lasts.

Education - *Mentor luck*

You have great Mentor Luck as you are surrounded by positive energies that attract all the right people who have your best interests at heart with no ulterior motives. These helpful souls make your life so fulfilling and pleasant, loaded with new experiences and sensations you never felt before.

ENHANCER FOR THE MONTH: The Sheep really benefits from the **Dragon Heavenly Seal Amulet** this month. This activates the precious Heaven Star #6 and attracts powerful support from the Deities. Great for those in business needing to close deals, but all Sheep could do with the helping hand of heaven behind them.

7th Month
Aug 8th - Sept 7th 2021

MISFORTUNE STAR ARRIVES. DO LITTLE THIS MONTH.

The unwelcome winds of the Five Yellow blow into your chart, but it is only a passing wind, so no need to get too worried. You get afflicted with all sorts of small but irksome illnesses, while your energy is also at a low ebb which makes things seem worse than they are. Wealth luck is not great so no surprises if you get into some kind of a cash bind. Don't overspend on luxuries because unexpected expenses may crop up. Make sure your medical insurance is up to date. For now, success seems distant and unattainable. You find it hard to get anything done and friends seem reluctant to help. You can lose physical things that are dear to you, as well as money. Avoid taking financial risks and leave the stock market alone as any speculative investments will not work out.

Work & Career - *Watch your back*

Watch your back at work. Although on the surface everyone appears friendly, you don't know what they are really thinking or their true agenda. Watch what you say and beware who you take into your confidence.

Better not share your genuine beliefs if controversial. There's every chance that what you say in jest can be used against you. Stay in control of potentially negative situations by focusing on your work. Outperform yourself and this will take you further than matching politics with politics. The more straightforward you are, the less at risk you will be of having to deal with office intrigues.

If someone is being overly nice, you can be sure there's an ulterior motive. There are plenty of wolves in sheep's clothing.

Business - *Poor judgement*
It is always better to lie low when your luck is not strong. The misfortune star weakens you, causing you to make unwise decisions. If you have someone you can rely on to formulate strategy, it may be smart to go with their judgement instead. Not a good time to introduce new strategies. Focus on your core business and build on what you have. Avoid risk-taking. If an investment has gone bad, it may be best to cut your losses. Don't throw good money after bad. Hold back on going into business with new partners, as you could end up being cheated. Postpone important decisions to next month as your judgment seems to be off.

Love & Relationships - *Don't be antagonistic*
You're not feeling your best and you tend to adopt a rather negative outlook. This could have a knock-on

effect on your relationship, causing misunderstandings to arise. Be more patient or the month could become rather bumpy for your social and love life. You are more antagonistic than usual and things could get out of hand if you're not careful. Avoid sensitive topics in conversation and try to see the other side's point of view.

Home & Family - *Unexpected expenses*

You don't feel particularly familial yet are forced to fork out more money due to unexpected expenses you didn't bargain for. This may strain your finances and put you in a lousy mood, especially if someone else causes the damage but you are left to pick up the bill. Don't be too grumpy as they are your blood kin. The extra costs may be in the form of home renovations, new fixtures or costly repairs for electrical items in the home.

Education - *Take it easy*

Not a great month all round, and it is the same for the Sheep in school. Those on summer break should count yourself lucky. If at school and things are not going your way, it's just the energies of the month. Things improve next month.

CURE FOR THE MONTH: Carry the **Five Element Pagoda with Tree of Life Amulet** to keep the *wu wang* at bay. This is important as the Five Yellow has a real ability to cause a lot of trouble.

8th Month
Sept 8th - Oct 7th 2021

RELATIONSHIPS FLOURISH. ROMANCE LUCK.

You amaze even yourself by the number of new friends you make in the coming month and many can be considered good friends. This is what will dominate your days this month. Relationships take up a much bigger chunk of your time, and for the Sheep, this is absolutely fine as you are a sociable creature at heart. You revel in your newfound popularity and others get enthralled by your captivating personality and lively conversation. Those looking for love find it easily. Call it romance for now, but if you are looking for something more permanent, the ball is in your court. This is also a great time for students.

Work & Career - *Articulate*

It is more talk than action this month but in a nice way. You do lots of talking but others are mesmerized by the way you express your thoughts and suggestions. You are articulate and composed to the extreme. You overflow with charisma to win even the most difficult person over to your side. Your powers of persuasion reach an all-time high so you might as well start by working on your boss. Earn his or her approval, then put your magic to work on clients and associates. You are in line to be promoted or receive a pay increase. Things are looking up for the Sheep chasing career success.

A series of happy coincidences allow you to prosper and assert your authority with minimal effort.

Business - *Networking brings benefits*
Successful networking nets you immense benefits and out of proportion rewards, so work on this! Life gets easier as new opportunities come from several sources. Someone you meet casually may be very beneficial so follow up on new leads. Sometimes chance encounters or an innocent phone call to touch base can have a major role to play in your life - this could well turn out to be the case this month. A good time to pursue growth and expansion strategies. Feel free to go with your instincts, because your instincts are good this month. Don't get overly concerned with detailed facts and numbers, as sometimes they hide more than they reveal. Use this month to formulate big picture plans; the details can come later.

Love & Relationships - *Finding love*
This month is devoted to love and passion so expect loads of romance enveloping you. Cupid definitely has his arrows aimed at you, while Venus seems to make

you the object of desire. Single Sheep have a ball playing the field as your sex appeal is at its apex. Whether in designer gear or the cheapest T and jeans, you ooze sex appeal and appear endlessly fascinating. You seem unable to go far wrong. You have the pick of the crop so take your time to find your soulmate. True love usually appears when you least expect it, but when it does, you will recognize it.

Family & Marriage - *Temptation*

Not surprisingly with so much temptation around, married Sheep may stray if their spouse is inattentive. This is poor excuse to have extra-marital affairs but even the most happily married among you may be persuaded to consider a casual fling by seducers. It is best to resist as you could regret this for a long time.

CURE FOR THE MONTH: Wear the **Double Happiness symbol** and keep a pair of **Marriage Happiness Ducks** in the SW of your home. This will protect your marriage and help ensure you have no reason to want to look outside of it for excitement.

Education - *Sociable*

Your social life is hectic to the point it may affect your studies. Having a good time with your mates seems to be more important than knuckling down to assignments; more so now when studies continue to be easy. But as long as when the time comes to buckle down, you do then, by all means have fun.

9th Month
Oct 8th - Nov 6th 2021

A HEATED & QUARRELSOME MONTH. BEWARE LAWSUITS.

The main concern will be your temper. You don't suffer fools gladly but just because you think you are smarter does not mean you are right. Be more tolerant as what comes around goes around. To all the world, the Sheep is usually viewed as a docile character, the ultimate diplomat. But when the anger of a Sheep gets unleashed, even the Tiger will cower. Do not let things get so out of hand that you damage relationships beyond repair. Beware of getting into trouble with the authorities, because the fines will not be lenient. Some could face lawsuits, so do be careful.

Work & Career - *Challenges*

There are many challenges to face at work. As well as being more bad-tempered, working to deadlines are likely to get you down. You may feel what is expected of you is unfair. Running the rat race was never something for the faint hearted, so if you are serious about making it somewhere in your career, you need to put yourself in the right frame of mind. Resist the temptation to feel sorry for yourself. If others seem to pick on you, blame it on your unfavourable astrological chart. Do not retaliate or let your adversaries annoy you. Ignore them, or even better, win them over onto your side.

Business - *Beware the law*

You may find those in authority seem to make it their business to make life difficult for you. Do not risk being penalized for no reason. If there are licenses or permits you need to have, be sure you have them well in advance. Do not be sloppy when it comes to the law. Straying from it will have you caught out, because that's the way the hand is dealt this month. Pay attention to details. There may be staff issues to deal with. Beware the disgruntled employee; he or she can make life more difficult than you think. Focus attention on making sure everyone who works for you is happy. It may be necessary to dig beneath the surface to see what is really going on. As long as you make the effort to find out, you won't uncover anything that is unsolvable.

Because business luck is not terribly promising, keep a watch on expenditures.

Love & Relationships - *Noisy*

A difficult month with relationships, especially the new ones just starting to develop. There is too much quarrelsome chi hovering, so anyone you are with will seem more disagreeable than usual. Don't be surprised if you and your partner are at each other's throats all the time. As long as your arguments don't turn into cold wars, things will work themselves out. Try not to be too serious. Learn to laugh things off!

Home & Family - *Full of yourself*

You may be rather full of yourself, making you difficult to hold a conversation with. Try to be less self-centered and you will find others better disposed towards you. Family matters are not utmost in your priorities, which may be a good thing, because if you cannot keep your mood under control, you stand to affect the harmony of the whole household by picking unnecessary fights.

Education - *Don't be a rebel*

Do not expect things to be easy this month. Resist falling into bad company and turning into a rebel. There's nothing to be gained from being difficult or defiant. Breaking rules may give you a high while doing it, but is certainly not worth the price you pay if you're caught.

CURE FOR THE MONTH: Carry the **Apple Peace Amulet** to calm the difficult energies this month. This will improve all your relationships and ensure you do not get into trouble with the law or authorities.

10th Month
Nov 7th - Dec 6th 2021

ILLNESS STAR SAPS YOU OF ENERGY

This is a low-energy, high-pressure month, and the illness star has made its way into your chart. This is sure to make you feel sluggish and exhausted, with little energy to pursue all the daunting tasks looming ahead. Avoid mental overload by planning your schedule well. Include some rest and relaxation time each day. Avoid high stress situations so you don't end up a nervous wreck. This is a lie-low kind of month where it is good to reduce your levels of responsibility. Unfortunately, the way your stars are lined up, it looks difficult to shirk off your commitments. If you need, ask for help. Don't try to do everything yourself. Look after your health - especially the more elderly Sheep. Remember to social distance, and take health concerns seriously.

Work & Career - *Don't overexert*

Your mental and physical state is weak. You are wallowing in the doldrums so you should not work long hours nor exert yourself too much, since body and soul cannot take it. Work smart and fill in your day with productive results. Do not slave over little details that do not count much. Allow others in and don't bother about claiming credit. You need assistance to get the jobs done! Having the right people on your side will do wonders and benefit your career now and in the near future. Relationship luck is strong, and this is a good time to get to know your co-workers better as they open up to you. You feel weak but you still wield some power; watch you don't let your arrogance get the better of you.

You need much goodwill these days, so appearing modest and less self-serving will be a start.

Business - *Avoid hasty reactions*
Be bold with your plans as fortune favours the bold this month. But being bold is not the same as being reckless so differentiate between the two! You can get carried away by the first signs of success and think you can start laughing all the way to the bank. Still, you can take some risks as you are particularly investment savvy now, so chances are high that whatever you touch can turn gold. Money luck is with you but you should focus on just one or two biggies. If you spread yourself too thin, you may not have the energy to see them through. Having projects stuck halfway is much worse than having nothing since they may return to haunt you or threaten you with more monetary outlay. Strangers are no-go; trust those you know for years since newcomers seem rather shady unless you know exactly where they stand. They may seem genuine and come up with tempting

offers but ask yourself why they are so nice to you when they hardly know you either!

Love & Relationships - *Love is everywhere!*

Love is everywhere you look, and you don't have to search too hard! You could find your true love at this time, so be open to new relationships. Be receptive to people and enjoy the attention showered on you. Single Sheep should take time to go out and mingle. Those already in a relationship should consider getting hitched as the person appears to be the one for you. No need scouting for others for comparison! Married Sheep are also in line for passion. However long you have been married, old sparks are easily ignited again. You just have to light it.

Education - *Steady up*

You may be feeling under the weather, dampening your motivation. Revision seems a drag. Work at your own pace, even if it takes longer. At least there will be fewer mistakes! Don't push yourself over the cliff; you will finish that assignment as long as you give yourself enough time, so don't drive yourself nuts!

CURE FOR THE MONTH: This month the Sheep gets very afflicted by the Illness Star. Carry **Medicine Buddha's Health Amulet** and keep **Vairocana** close to protect against contagious diseases.

11th Month
Dec 7th - Jan 5th 2022

VICTORY LUCK HELPS YOU OVERCOME THE COMPETITION

This is a transformational month! Things mutate before your eyes and usually for the better so you can sleep easy. Luck blooms from all sides and good things come in droves! As this period is an important period of change, it is not a time for indecision. You must decide which steps to take to come up with an informed opinion. Luckily, you make mostly good decisions. If you have been sitting on the fence, now is the time to take the bull by the horns and let your voice be heard. It is also necessary as you can't move ahead unless you take a stand. Others simply cannot do it for you. This period augurs well for new ventures, so get cracking on ideas you've been working on. You have winning luck, so don't let a little competition faze you; let it inspire you to do better.

Work & Career - *Promotion luck*

Expect changes in the workplace, but nothing too traumatic to worry about. In fact, there is good news, since there is a chance of a promotion. However, this is the sort that comes without fanfare or hullabaloo, so keep a low profile and don't make a song and dance about it. Do your work well and be quietly confident. Any outward showiness may ruin your chances. Impress by delivering the goods, not by talking yourself up and out!

A lucky month when you have a real edge over the competition. In fact, the more competitive a situation, the sharper you become.

Business - *New directions*

Success comes when you expand your contacts. Don't stick to your peers in the same industry even if you feel most relaxed with them. The more diverse the people you know, the better, since opportunities come in different shapes, sizes and industries! Actively build your social and business base. Go through your name cards. Call if you have an urge even if you think they may waste your time.

This month you learn a lot from casual, random conversations, so stay sharp. Invest in and read the daily newspapers. Read from cover to cover, even the non-business sections. Be well-read and well-informed so during social gatherings, you will be able to stand your own. Be bold in investing, expanding and launching new initiatives. Your luck here holds strong and plans set in motion now bring rich rewards later. This is the time to consider moving in new directions you thought were alien to your knowledge.

Love & Relationships - *Long-term*

Things are solid on the love front. You command attention and are surrounded by admirers willing to submit, but you're not in the mood for casual flings. You are more interested in something with long-term potential. If you look, there are many candidates; no need to be in a hurry to pick one. Take your time and enjoy! Married Sheep reach a new level in their relationship with their spouses.

Education - *Sterling*

You deliver sterling results and your performance is the envy of all. You have outstanding relationships with your teachers, who vouch for you if you're looking to write college applications. Those who have been putting in the work will see it start to pay off handsomely. You display obvious leadership and others recognize this by nominating you to head some club, society or event.

ENHANCER FOR THE MONTH: Boost good fortune luck this month with the **Victory Banner Success Amulet**.

12th Month
Jan 6th - Feb 3rd 2022

MOVING GALLANTLY INTO THE NEW YEAR

The Sheep moves into the Year of the Tiger with plenty of power and energy. A time when one good thing leads to another. After last month's go-getting adventures that saw you scaling new heights, the juggernaut continues with a period of intensified energy. You are even more revved up this month as things happen at a faster pace. Luckily you are more than able to keep up so life is busy and happy. You are keen to be knee-deep with everything that is going on around you and you struggle to find time to fit all that interests you! Your success generates envy so this may be the time when you discover who your real friends are, and who are fair-weather people.

Work & Career - *Plot and scheme if you must*

You are keeping very busy at work but that is just how you like it. There may be office politics to contend with but nothing you cannot handle. If things get too hot for comfort, you should turn the tables and let them get a taste of their own medicine. Be clever about doing this and let the world think you are the victim deserving sympathy. You can scheme as well as any of your rivals! But maintain your integrity. Help your colleagues if asked; anyone can do with extra goodwill though you seem unassailable now. The more allies you have, the stronger your bargaining power. Since you are so successful, you can afford to help others when you are top dog, but make sure they know whose debt they owe!

A month of nonstop action and you have the energy, drive and stamina for it! The best way to close out the year and to get ready for a new one!

Business - *Long-term prospects*
Be daring. If you have new ideas, put them into motion even if some people think they are wacky. The really different tactics could be the ones that work like a charm, propelling your business to exciting new levels! But beware public quarrels and open hostility if confronted with difficult clients or dirty competition. Do not retort or air dirty laundry in public. Anything reckless said in the heat of the moment may have bad repercussions. With things moving so fast, take time to strategise instead of simply going with the flow, which may be tempting. You may need to consciously slow down as your mind seems to be working overtime. This is also a fortuitous time to invest in research and development.

Love & Relationships - *Move fast*

You're full of energy and attract the same kind of people into your life. Those looking for romance find it quickly and it promises to be a whirlwind ride. You exude a natural charm and others are happy to fall in with your plans. You are also a hopeless romantic, and your positive attitude rubs off on others. If you find someone you think you have a real future with, move fast. This is a good window of opportunity for you to make your move.

Home & Family - *Time for bonding*

Lots of positive energy at home means that the more time you spend with your family, the more you enjoy. Family bonding is important to you now and you are perfectly happy to be with your kin even at the expense of socializing. Parents with young children find this period spent with their offspring particularly rewarding.

Education - *Excellent*

You have instant rapport with anyone with something to teach you because you are thirsty for knowledge. This makes you the dream student as long as you stay interested. Make the most of this time to make that quantum jump to the next level. Those sitting exams now are likely to do very well.

ENHANCER FOR THE MONTH: The Sheep benefits from the **Crimson Phoenix Lunar Mansion Talisman** this month.

for more on all the recommended
feng shui cures, remedies & enhancers for

2021

please log on to

www.fsmegamall.com/2021

for more on feng shui, visit

www.wofs.com